liv b's
easy everyday

LIV B'S EASY everyday

100 Sheet-Pan, One-Pot and 5-Ingredient Vegan Recipes

olivia biermann

Robert
ROSE

Liv B's Easy Everyday

Library and Archives Canada Cataloguing in Publication
Title: Liv B's easy everyday : 100 sheet-pan, one-pot and 5-ingredient vegan recipes / Olivia Biermann.
Other titles: Easy everyday | 100 sheet-pan, one-pot and 5-ingredient vegan recipes | One hundred sheet-pan, one-pot and five-ingredient vegan recipes
Names: Biermann, Olivia, 1994- author.
Description: Includes index.
Identifiers: Canadiana 20210094982 | ISBN 9780778806790 (softcover)
Subjects: LCSH: Vegan cooking. | LCSH: Quick and easy cooking. | LCGFT: Cookbooks.
Classification: LCC TX837 .B49 2021 | DDC 641.5/6362—dc23

Disclaimer
The recipes in this book have been carefully tested by our kitchen and our tasters. To the best of our knowledge, they are safe and nutritious for ordinary use and users. For those people with food or other allergies, or who have special food requirements or health issues, please read the suggested contents of each recipe carefully and determine whether or not they may create a problem for you. All recipes are used at the risk of the consumer.

We cannot be responsible for any hazards, loss or damage that may occur as a result of any recipe use.

For those with special needs, allergies, requirements or health problems, in the event of any doubt, please contact your medical adviser prior to the use of any recipe.

Art Direction: Margaux Keres
Cover and book design: Margaux Keres
Cover and interior photography: Ashley Lima
Additional photography
(pages 8, 12, 73, 81, 134, 166, 216): Greg Bellefontaine
Editor: Meredith Dees
Copyeditor & Indexer: Gillian Watts
Proofreader: Kelly Jones
Food Styling: Ashley Lima
Prop Styling: Ashley Lima & Margaux Keres

The publisher gratefully acknowledges the financial support of our publishing program by the Government of Canada through the Canada Book Fund.

Canadä

Published by Robert Rose Inc.
120 Eglinton Avenue East, Suite 800, Toronto, Ontario, Canada M4P 1E2
Tel: (416) 322-6552 Fax: (416) 322-6936
www.robertrose.ca

Printed and bound in Canada

1 2 3 4 5 6 7 8 9 SO 29 28 27 26 25 24 23 22 21

To my family and friends,
who never fail to make me
laugh, support my dreams
and eat my food

table of contents

introduction

Cooking and baking have been part of my life for as long as I can remember. My earliest baking memory is from when I was six. I remember stirring a small package of brownie mix with water and popping it into my Easy-Bake Oven, which basically cooked food with a light bulb. I sliced that single-serving brownie into four pieces, decorated each with icing sugar, then forced my family to sit at the table, where I served them their tiny portion, feeling so very proud of myself.

I loved helping my mom bake cookies almost every Sunday afternoon (by then in a real oven, thank goodness), stirring a pot of spaghetti sauce and learning how to make rice. By the time I was 11, I would prepare my own packed lunches for the next school day and wake up early to make elaborate breakfasts before catching the bus.

It might seem odd to some, but learning how to cook has been one of the most meaningful experiences of my life. When I went vegan, I had to make more of my meals at home, since restaurant options were limited back then — and I was a student on a tight budget!

When I began writing this book in early 2020, I could not have anticipated what was going to unfold in the coming months. As the world shut down, people stockpiled and stayed home, quickly becoming burnt out from juggling work and family. With takeout options initially nonexistent, knowing how to cook was a major blessing. I knew immediately that I wanted to create a plant-based cookbook that would make people's lives easier. Everything in these pages was conceived with simplicity in mind. All the recipes are either five-ingredient or cooked in one pot or on a sheet pan, to free up time and help you simplify your life too. And, as always, I'm conscious of the cost.

In a world of seemingly endless tasks, to-do lists and people clamoring for our attention, it's no wonder so many of us don't have the time or energy to cook. I really hope this book will give you some inspiration to get into the kitchen.

— Liv

about the book

This book uses three icons: to indicate five-ingredient, one-pot and sheet-pan recipes. There are so many cookbooks out there that claim to be simple or easy but, upon further inspection, contain complicated directions and crazy-long ingredient lists. My goal has always been to show people how easy and delicious vegan food can be. Below you will find a description for each icon so you'll know what to expect when you see them throughout the book.

icons

 ONE POT These recipes are generally cooked in one pot on the stove or in an electric pressure cooker (such as an Instant Pot), or prepared in one mixing bowl.

 5-INGREDIENT These recipes all use five ingredients or fewer, with the exception of water, a little salt and pepper (staples in most households) and a small amount of oil for frying, roasting or greasing a bowl. These recipes are just as delicious as any of the others in the book, but they use fewer ingredients so you can save time and money on preparation.

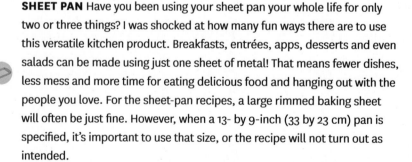 **SHEET PAN** Have you been using your sheet pan your whole life for only two or three things? I was shocked at how many fun ways there are to use this versatile kitchen product. Breakfasts, entrées, apps, desserts and even salads can be made using just one sheet of metal! That means fewer dishes, less mess and more time for eating delicious food and hanging out with the people you love. For the sheet-pan recipes, a large rimmed baking sheet will often be just fine. However, when a 13- by 9-inch (33 by 23 cm) pan is specified, it's important to use that size, or the recipe will not turn out as intended.

equipment

I'm all about keeping things simple and minimal when possible, and that extends to my cooking as well. Though I have a well-stocked kitchen, I definitely don't go overboard with single-use gadgets and utensils I don't need. For the majority of the recipes in this book, you won't need more than a few common kitchen tools. If you're like me and try to buy only things that you will use a lot and that will really cut down on time and effort while cooking, these are great to have on hand:

AIRTIGHT CONTAINERS AND JARS I love meal prepping and leftovers, so having different sizes of containers and jars makes storing food for later so easy and convenient!

BLENDER A blender is one of my most-used kitchen tools. Splurging on a high-powered blender is definitely worth it if you blend as much as I do. I use it for smoothies, sauces and even homemade nut butters. However, there are many recipes in this book that a regular blender can handle just fine.

COFFEE TOOLS As a coffee lover (see pages 49 to 54), having an espresso machine and a quality milk frother makes my daily cup so enjoyable, not to mention quick to make. Disregard this suggestion if you don't drink coffee!

FRYING PANS I have a few different sizes and types of frying pans, but a large pan is most often my go-to, and what you'll need to cook my recipes.

RIMMED BAKING SHEETS Baking sheets are essential for many recipes in this book. Having a few on hand will take you far: you can roast, bake and even prepare entire meals on one — the list is endless, really. Don't forget that a quarter sheet pan (13 by 9 inches/33 by 23 cm) is needed for some of the recipes in this book.

MIXING BOWLS Large mixing bowls are ideal for combining ingredients when baking or for breading cauliflower, tofu or seitan. I prefer small mixing bowls for making sauces and dressings.

POTS Large pots are great for soups, curries and pasta, and small pots are helpful when you're cooking for one or making just a tiny amount of something.

ingredients

As with kitchen tools, I don't love going overboard on ingredients. I try to favor those that get used a lot, so you don't end up buying something you use once and then it sits on your shelf for a year, until maybe you make that recipe again. That being said, having these staple pantry ingredients on hand will help as you cook your way through the chapters of this book:

CANNED GOODS & SAUCES Beans (cannellini and chickpeas), canned tomatoes, full-fat coconut milk, lentils, low-sodium vegetable broth, marinara sauce, pure maple syrup and reduced-sodium soy sauce can be used for many recipes in this book, and they are fairly inexpensive to stock up on.

OILS Oils are a great shelf-stable essential to have on hand. I always have three in my pantry: vegetable oil for frying, olive oil for dressings and sauces, and coconut oil for baking and frying.

GRAINS Short-grain white or brown rice and wheat pasta are my go-tos, but I often have quinoa in my pantry too. They are essential for meal prep, batch cooking and quick weeknight meals.

NUTS, SEEDS & BUTTERS I always have a big jar of almond butter in my pantry, as well as a small jar of tahini. I prefer to make my own coconut butter (see page 32), because it's much cheaper than store-bought.

SPICES I love experimenting with spices, but I do use the same ones very often in my everyday cooking, on purpose. You can prepare a large majority of the recipes in this book with these common spices: chili powder, garlic powder, onion powder, salt, black pepper and dried Italian seasoning. Two specialty items I love to have on hand as well are smoked paprika and nutritional yeast, which I buy from my bulk food store.

sauces, spreads
& cheese

marvelous maple almond sauce

MAKES ½ CUP (125 ML) • **5** ⬤ • TIME: 5 MINUTES

In true Canadian fashion, I have a soft spot for maple anything. And as much as I love maple syrup, sometimes I like to do a little extra for certain occasions. A pancake brunch with your friends is even more fun when you serve this salted maple almond sauce instead of boring old maple syrup (just kidding . . . mostly). It's heavenly warmed up and drizzled over my Light & Fluffy Pancakes (page 63) or vanilla coconut milk ice cream (see my tip).

¼ cup (60 mL) pure maple syrup
¼ cup (60 mL) creamy almond butter

2 tbsp (30 mL) coconut oil
Pinch salt

1. Heat a small pot over medium heat. Add the maple syrup, almond butter, coconut oil and salt; stir to combine. Cook for about 5 minutes, stirring frequently, until warmed and starting to bubble slightly.

2. Remove from the heat and serve immediately. Store the leftovers in an airtight container or jar in the fridge for up to 1 week.

my tip To reheat this sauce, spoon it into a microwave-safe bowl and microwave on Medium in 20-second intervals, stirring in between, until warm and runny.

super-quick fresh tomato salsa

MAKES 2 CUPS (500 ML) · **5** ⬤ · TIME: 10 MINUTES

This recipe was inspired by the popular Mexican salsa pico de gallo (also known as salsa fresca). It's chunky and juicy and pairs well with many dishes, although I like it best on top of warm, cheesy nachos (page 96).

3 medium plum (Roma) tomatoes, diced
½ cup (125 mL) diced white onion
⅓ cup (75 mL) finely chopped fresh cilantro

2 tbsp (30 mL) freshly squeezed lime juice
Pinch salt

1. Combine the tomatoes, onion, cilantro, lime juice and salt in a medium bowl. Serve immediately or transfer to an airtight container and store in the fridge for up to 3 days.

spiced tahini sauce

MAKES ½ CUP (125 ML) • 🥣 • TIME: 5 MINUTES

This recipe was inspired by a basic tahini sauce that's popular throughout the Middle East and uses three main ingredients: tahini paste, lemon juice and garlic. You'll find it in many variations as a sauce for veggies, in salads or on sandwiches, just to name a few. I love to switch out the lemon juice for lime and add spices to the tahini base. Not only does it make the sauce a lovely golden brown color, it adds more kick too! This recipe is amazing as a dip for Crispy Garlic Parm Cauliflower Wings (page 90) or drizzled over Leftover Grains & Cauliflower Tray Bake (page 190).

⅓ cup (75 mL) creamy tahini
3 tbsp (45 mL) warm water
3 tbsp (45 mL) pure maple syrup
2 tbsp (30 mL) freshly squeezed lime juice
1 tbsp (15 mL) reduced-sodium soy sauce

¼ tsp (1 mL) onion powder
¼ tsp (1 mL) chili powder
¼ tsp (1 mL) ground cumin
⅛ tsp (0.5 mL) garlic powder

1. Place the tahini, water, maple syrup, lime juice, soy sauce, onion powder, chili powder, cumin and garlic powder in a small bowl; whisk to combine. Serve immediately or store in an airtight container or jar in the fridge for up to 1 week.

my tip This recipe can easily be doubled or tripled if you want to make a big batch to last the week. It will thicken in the fridge, so stir in up to 2 tbsp (30 mL) warm water, as needed, until the consistency is runny.

"honey" garlic sauce

MAKES ⅔ CUP (150 ML) • **5** • TIME: 10 MINUTES

This sauce was created for my "Honey" Garlic Tofu & Broccoli recipe (page 154), but it's amazing with vegetable stir-fries and vegan cauliflower wings as well. It tastes like a classic honey garlic sauce, but this version is made vegan by swapping out the honey for brown sugar.

¼ cup (60 mL) water, divided
2 tsp (10 mL) cornstarch
¼ cup (60 mL) lightly packed brown sugar

2 tbsp (30 mL) reduced-sodium soy sauce
1 tbsp (15 mL) white vinegar
4 garlic cloves, minced

1. Combine 1 tbsp (15 mL) water and cornstarch in a small bowl. Set aside.

2. Heat a small pot over medium heat. Add 3 tbsp (45 mL) water, brown sugar, soy sauce, vinegar and garlic; stir to combine. Bring to a simmer and cook, stirring frequently, for about 3 minutes.

3. Pour the cornstarch mixture into the pot; whisk immediately to combine. Bring to a simmer and cook, stirring occasionally, for 2 minutes, until the sauce has thickened but is still pourable.

4. Remove from the heat and serve immediately or store in an airtight container or jar in the fridge for up to 1 week.

my tip To reheat, place leftover sauce in a small pot over medium heat. Heat, stirring frequently, for about 5 minutes or until runny and warm. Alternatively, transfer to a microwave-safe bowl and microwave on Medium in 20-second intervals, stirring in between, until warm and runny.

basil & walnut pesto

MAKES 1 CUP (250 ML) •   • TIME: 10 MINUTES

Pesto is usually made with pine nuts, but they are extremely expensive, sometimes hard to find and can be limiting if you have an allergy. So I wanted to create a basic recipe that allows for some flexibility. I like to use walnuts here, but you can substitute a variety of different nuts or seeds, depending on availability or preference. This pesto is so tasty on my roasted tempeh bowl (page 149), pasta or pizza, or even just spread on crackers.

1 cup (250 mL) packed fresh basil leaves

½ cup (125 mL) raw walnuts (see my tips)

3 garlic cloves

2 tbsp (30 mL) freshly squeezed lemon juice

Pinch salt

½ cup (125 mL) extra-virgin olive oil

Food processor or high-powered blender

1. Place the basil, walnuts and garlic in the food processor. Pulse until finely chopped.

2. Add the lemon juice and salt. With the motor running, slowly pour in the olive oil. (This helps keep the oil from separating and makes it nice and creamy!) You may need to stop the motor periodically to scrape down the sides of the bowl.

3. Use immediately or store in an airtight container or jar in the fridge for up to 4 days.

my tips Feel free to substitute an equal amount of raw sunflower seeds, pumpkin seeds, pistachios, pine nuts or almonds for the walnuts.

Keep in mind that the pesto will oxidize and turn slightly brown on top in the fridge, but you can scoop off the top layer when you're ready to use it.

To freeze, scoop 1 tbsp (15 mL) pesto into the cups of an ice cube tray and freeze for about 4 hours, until solid. Transfer the frozen pesto cubes to an airtight container and store in the freezer for up to 6 months. This allows you to thaw only the exact amount you need for a recipe.

vegan buffalo sauce

MAKES ⅔ CUP (150 ML) •   • TIME: 10 MINUTES

Traditional Buffalo sauce is often just hot sauce, vinegar and butter. If you are vegan or avoiding dairy and thought you couldn't enjoy this much-loved pub staple, the great news is, you can! Use vegan butter and it will taste just like the real thing, I promise. You can also find this sauce in my Buffalo Chickpea Nachos (page 96) recipe, but I love it with Crispy Garlic Parm Cauliflower Wings too (see my tip).

½ cup (125 mL) cayenne pepper sauce, such as Frank's

¼ cup (60 mL) vegan butter

1 tsp (5 mL) white vinegar

⅛ tsp (0.5 mL) garlic powder

1. Heat a small pot over medium heat. Add the cayenne pepper sauce, vegan butter, vinegar and garlic powder; stir to combine. Cook, stirring frequently, for 3 minutes, until the butter has melted and the mixture is combined.

2. Remove from the heat and let cool slightly. Pour into a jar and store in an airtight container in the fridge for up to 1 week. The sauce will separate in the fridge, so shake vigorously for about 1 minute before using.

my tip Turn my Crispy Garlic Parm Cauliflower Wings (page 90) into Buffalo wings. Place the cooked wings in a large mixing bowl and drizzle 1 recipe Vegan Buffalo Sauce overtop. Toss gently to coat, then serve.

herb & garlic parmesan sprinkle

MAKES ¾ CUP (175 ML) • **5** 🔻 • TIME: 5 MINUTES

This recipe is cheesy, salty and herby, and it contains only dry pantry staples that you might already have on hand. You can use this sprinkle in any recipe that calls for vegan Parmesan cheese. Keep in mind that the mixture has a nice punch of garlic flavor, so if you're sprinkling it over something that already has a lot of garlic in it, you might want to omit the garlic powder.

1 cup (250 mL) raw sunflower seeds
¼ cup (60 mL) nutritional yeast
2 tsp (10 mL) dried Italian seasoning
1 tsp (5 mL) salt

¼ tsp (1 mL) garlic powder

Food processor or
high-powered blender

1. Place the sunflower seeds, nutritional yeast, Italian seasoning, salt and garlic powder in the food processor. Process for about 30 seconds, until it resembles powdered Parmesan cheese. Use immediately or store in an airtight container in the fridge for up to 2 weeks.

my tip If you want to add some kick to this sprinkle, add ⅛ to ¼ tsp (0.5 to 1 mL) cayenne pepper, depending on how much heat you like.

sunflower caesar dressing

MAKES 1 CUP (250 ML) • **5** 🍲 • **TIME: 5 MINUTES**

This dressing found its way into my weekly meal prep and now I can't believe how many things I use it for! Of course, I love it on my Kale & Brussels Caesar-esque Salad (page 120), but I've also used it as a dipping sauce for Crispy Garlic Parm Cauliflower Wings (page 90) and carrot sticks. It's creamy and perfectly tangy and has a lovely garlic flavor. You'll find that it tastes slightly nuttier than a traditional cashew cream sauce, but I love that it's nut-free.

1 cup (250 mL) water
½ cup (125 mL) raw sunflower seeds
1 tbsp (15 mL) Dijon mustard
1 tbsp (15 mL) apple cider vinegar

1 garlic clove
¼ tsp (1 mL) black pepper
Pinch salt

High-powered blender

1. Pour the water into a high-powered blender. Add the sunflower seeds, Dijon mustard, vinegar, garlic, pepper and salt; blend on high speed for about 1 minute, until smooth. Serve immediately or store in an airtight container in the fridge for up to 5 days.

mixed nut & seed butter

MAKES 2 CUPS (500 ML) • **5** 🍴 • TIME: 10 MINUTES

I love nut butter in my morning smoothies, so I wanted to create a homemade version with an interesting twist. This recipe is super convenient because you can use up smaller quantities of nuts you might have on hand. Feel free to substitute different types of nuts for the almonds; cashews, peanuts and pecans are all great choices.

1 cup (250 mL) raw sunflower seeds
1 cup (250 mL) raw pumpkin seeds

1 cup (250 mL) raw almonds

Food processor

1. Place the sunflower seeds, pumpkin seeds and almonds in a food processor. Process for about 8 to 10 minutes, until very smooth. You may need to stop the motor periodically to scrape down the sides of the bowl. Use immediately or store in an airtight container or jar in the fridge for up to 2 weeks.

> my tip You can also use roasted nuts in this recipe. I specify raw here because a lot of store-bought nuts are high in sodium, but if you like a bit of salty flavor, you can add a pinch of salt while processing.

almost-instant refrigerator berry jam

MAKES 1 CUP (250 ML) • 5 ⬤ • TIME: 15 MINUTES

The first jam I learned how to make required gelatin (a non-vegan ingredient) and a good hour of simmering time, not to mention all the hassle of sterilizing jars. This refrigerator jam requires only four ingredients, 15 minutes and one clean, airtight container or jar. It might seem unusual to include chia seeds in jam, but they are a popular vegan thickener and add a boost of healthy fats too. See my tips for additional flavor combinations.

2 cups (500 mL) fresh or frozen strawberries, raspberries or blueberries, or a combination

2 tbsp (30 mL) chia seeds
1 tbsp (15 mL) orange juice
1 tbsp (15 mL) organic cane sugar

1. Heat a medium pot over medium heat. Add the strawberries; cook for about 5 minutes, stirring frequently, until the juices have been released. Remove from the heat and use a potato masher or fork to gently break down the berries, until relatively smooth.

2. Return the pot to medium heat. Add the chia seeds, orange juice and sugar; stir to combine. Cook for 5 minutes, stirring frequently, until thickened. Remove from the heat and let cool completely before serving (it will continue to thicken as it cools). Store in an airtight container or jar in the fridge for up to 1 week.

my tips Once you've mastered the recipe above, try one of these fancy combinations: **STRAWBERRY BASIL JAM** Use only strawberries in Step 1 and add 1 tbsp (15 mL) minced fresh basil in Step 2. **BLUEBERRY VANILLA JAM** Use only blueberries in Step 1 and add 1 tsp (5 mL) vanilla extract in Step 2.

creamy coconut butter

MAKES 1 CUP (250 ML) •   • TIME: 15 MINUTES

I first tried coconut butter after buying a jar at a health food store. It's thick, creamy and spreadable like a nut butter, but it tastes like pure coconut. Now I save money and make my own, which is easy and more cost-effective, since the store-bought version often comes with a hefty price tag! I love using coconut butter in sweet recipes, like adding a heaping spoonful to my oatmeal, and as a vegan butter substitute in my Gluten-Free Coconut Butter Brownies (page 209).

4 cups (1 L) unsweetened shredded coconut

1 tbsp (15 mL) melted coconut oil

Food processor or high-powered blender

1. Place the shredded coconut in a food processor. Process for about 5 minutes, until it becomes a thick, clumpy ball. You may need to stop the motor periodically to scrape down the sides of the bowl.

2. Add the coconut oil. Process for about 5 minutes, until the consistency is thick but pourable. Use immediately or store in an airtight container or jar at room temperature for up to 2 weeks (see my tips).

my tips Homemade coconut butter will be slightly grainy no matter how long you process it. This is totally fine!

If the temperature of your home is on the colder side, the coconut butter can harden at room temperature. Place the jar or container in a shallow pot of hot water and it will soften. Alternatively, if you're using it on hot food such as oatmeal, scrape out the amount you wish to use and it will melt quite quickly.

vanilla buttercream

In my opinion, everyone needs to know how to make frosting. Sure, you can buy it from the store, but where's the fun in that? This vanilla "buttercream" has become a staple in my kitchen for holidays, birthdays and "just because" Sunday-afternoon baking.

3 cups (750 mL) confectioners' (icing) sugar, divided

⅓ cup (75 mL) vegan butter, softened

¼ cup (60 mL) unsweetened nondairy milk

1 tsp (5 mL) vanilla extract

Electric mixer

1. Combine 1 cup (250 mL) confectioners' sugar, vegan butter, nondairy milk and vanilla in a large bowl.

2. Using an electric mixer, beat for about 1 minute, until smooth. Add the remaining confectioners' sugar, ½ cup (125 mL) at a time, then beat for about 2 minutes, until smooth. Use immediately or store in an airtight container in the fridge for up to 5 days.

my tip Frosting can also be frozen! Simply store in an airtight container in the freezer for up to 3 months. To reuse, place the container in the fridge to thaw overnight.

classic chocolate frosting

MAKES 1½ CUPS (375 ML) •   • TIME: 10 MINUTES

There are a few recipes my mom made sure my sister and I knew before we moved out, and one was a good classic chocolate frosting. Being an avid baker when I was younger, I had pretty much mastered this frosting recipe by age 11 (fortunately, that didn't mean my mom thought I was leaving home at 12!). I continue to make the same recipe to this day, with a few substitutions to make it vegan. This is perfect on cakes, cupcakes and my Gluten-Free Coconut Butter Brownies (page 209).

2½ cups (625 mL) confectioners' (icing) sugar, divided

¼ cup (60 mL) vegan margarine or vegan butter, softened

¼ cup (60 mL) unsweetened cocoa powder

3 tbsp (45 mL) unsweetened nondairy milk

2 tsp (10 mL) vanilla extract

Electric mixer

1. Combine 1 cup (250 mL) confectioners' sugar, vegan margarine, cocoa powder, nondairy milk and vanilla in a large bowl.

2. Using an electric mixer, beat for 1 minute, until smooth. Add the remaining confectioners' sugar, ½ cup (125 mL) at a time; then beat for 2 minutes, until smooth. Use immediately or store in an airtight container in the fridge for up to 5 days.

my tip To freeze, store in an airtight container in the freezer for up to 3 months. To reuse, place the container in the fridge and thaw overnight until ready to use.

beverages

good morning green juice

SERVES 1 • **5** • TIME: 5 MINUTES

When it comes to juice, I think most people default to store-bought. However, making your own juice at home is easy, fun and can save you money! Feel free to modify the ingredients in this recipe as you please. For example, to make the juice sweeter, add more apple. Or to give it more of a kick, double the ginger.

½ cup (125 mL) water
2 green apples, quartered
2 cups (500 mL) baby spinach or chopped kale, ribs removed
1 English cucumber, chopped

½ inch (1 cm) piece ginger, peeled
½ cup (125 mL) ice cubes

Blender
Nut milk bag, cheesecloth or French press coffee maker (see my tips)

1. Pour the water into a blender. Add the apple, spinach, cucumber, ginger and ice; blend on high speed for 30 to 40 seconds, until smooth.

2. Strain the mixture through a nut milk bag into a jar or container to remove the pulp. Discard the pulp. (See my tips for the cheesecloth and French press methods.)

3. Pour into a glass or store, covered, in the refrigerator for up to 3 days. The juice will separate, so make sure to shake well before drinking.

my tips If you don't have a nut milk bag, you can use either of the following two methods to strain the juice: **CHEESECLOTH METHOD** Line a fine-mesh sieve with a double layer of cheesecloth, then strain the juice into a jar or container. **FRENCH PRESS METHOD** Pour the juice into the French press, then slowly push down on the plunger. Pour into a glass or container and enjoy or save for later!

chocolate espresso smoothie

SERVES 1 • **5** 🔻 • TIME: 10 MINUTES

I have a newfound love for coffee, so I wanted to try combining it with my first love — smoothies! This one is my go-to when I'm in a rush in the morning and don't have time to make breakfast and coffee. The protein powder is key here: it will keep you full longer and help you avoid the coffee jitters.

1 cup (250 mL) unsweetened nondairy milk

2 tbsp (30 mL) brewed espresso or strong brewed coffee

1 frozen banana, chopped

1 serving chocolate vegan protein powder

1 tbsp (15 mL) almond butter or peanut butter (optional)

3 ice cubes

High-powered blender

1. Pour the nondairy milk and espresso into a high-powered blender. Add the banana, vegan protein powder, almond butter (if using) and ice cubes; blend on high speed for about 1 minute, until smooth.

2. Pour into a glass and drink immediately.

creamsicle in a cup

SERVES 1 • **5** • TIME: 5 MINUTES
(PLUS 2 HOURS FOR FREEZING)

As a kid, I loved the classic Creamsicle combination of orange and vanilla. At summer camp we used to have Creamsicles in the afternoon, and I remember how funny it was to have ice cream melting all over our hands as we rushed to finish eating them! I love this smoothie because the flavors remind me of such fun times growing up.

3 tbsp (45 mL) full-fat coconut milk (see my tip)

1 cup (250 mL) orange juice

1 serving vanilla vegan protein powder

½ cup (125 mL) frozen mango chunks or chopped frozen banana

High-powered blender

1. Pour 1 tbsp (15 mL) coconut milk into each of 3 cups of an ice cube tray. Freeze for at least 2 hours, until solid.

2. Pour the orange juice into a high-powered blender. Add the coconut milk cubes, vegan protein powder and mango. Blend on high speed for 1 minute, until smooth.

3. Pour into a glass and drink immediately.

my tip If you wish to make more coconut milk cubes, fill the entire ice cube tray and freeze until solid. Pop them out of the tray and transfer to a freezer-safe container or bag. Store in the freezer for up to 3 months and use as needed from frozen. These cubes are also great for hot recipes too! Toss 2 or 3 into a pot of soup or curry to add a bit of extra creaminess.

everyday green smoothie

SERVES 1 · **5** ⬤ · TIME: 5 MINUTES

It's not often that I find a green smoothie recipe I want to stick with. I used to just throw whatever ingredients I had on hand into the blender and hope for the best. However, since discovering this creamy, dreamy smoothie combo, I find myself coming back to it again and again. Bonus: it's banana-free, for all you banana haters!

1 cup (250 mL) unsweetened nondairy milk

1 cup (250 mL) lightly packed baby spinach

¾ cup (175 mL) frozen mango chunks (see my tip)

1 tbsp (15 mL) hemp seeds

1 tbsp (15 mL) chia seeds

High-powered blender

1. Pour the nondairy milk into a high-powered blender. Add the spinach, mango, hemp seeds and chia seeds; blend on high speed for about 1 minute, until smooth.

2. Pour into a glass and drink immediately.

my tip Sometimes frozen mango is hard to blend because the chunks are often large. I like to let the fruit thaw for 5 minutes before blending, so my blender doesn't have to work as hard.

banana bread smoothie

SERVES 1 · **5** · TIME: 5 MINUTES

If you've read my first book, you'll know I'm pretty obsessed with banana bread, and so are my YouTube subscribers! One of my most popular recipe videos is for banana bread, which is why I decided to make a banana bread–inspired smoothie recipe.

1 cup (250 mL) vanilla nondairy milk
1 frozen banana, chopped
2 tbsp (30 mL) raw walnuts

1 tbsp (15 mL) pure maple syrup
¼ tsp (1 mL) ground cinnamon

High-powered blender

1. Pour the nondairy milk into a high-powered blender. Add the banana, walnuts, maple syrup and cinnamon; blend on high speed for 1 minute, until smooth.

2. Pour into a glass and drink immediately.

my tip If you prefer a thicker smoothie, add up to 3 ice cubes.

best-ever berry smoothie

SERVES 1 · **5** ⬤ · TIME: 5 MINUTES

This smoothie is the best breakfast or pre-workout drink! Using an unsweetened nondairy milk cuts down on sweetness, allowing the natural flavors of the berries to shine. I add a spoonful of nut butter to make it creamy and also to add some healthy fat.

1 cup (250 mL) unsweetened nondairy milk
½ cup (125 mL) frozen mixed berries
1 ripe banana

1 tbsp (15 mL) almond butter
Pinch ground cinnamon

Blender

1. Pour the nondairy milk into a blender. Add the berries, banana, almond butter and cinnamon; blend on high speed for 1 minute, until smooth.

2. Pour into a glass and drink immediately.

> my tip To make this even more filling, add a scoop of your favorite vegan protein powder in Step 1.

liv's classic iced latte

SERVES 1 · **5** · TIME: 5 MINUTES

Coffee was never on my radar until about a year ago (how did I manage 24 years without it?). I don't remember why I decided to try it, but it was pretty much love at first sip. When it comes to hot coffee drinks, I love them as sweet as possible. But in the summer, when I'm craving an iced latte, I prefer the coffee flavor to be more pronounced, so I make it with a sweetened nut milk and don't add extra sugar.

1 cup (250 mL) ice cubes
1 cup (250 mL) sweetened nondairy milk

2 tbsp (30 mL) brewed espresso
or strong brewed coffee

1. Place the ice cubes in a large glass. Pour in the nondairy milk, then the espresso. Stir until combined and enjoy immediately.

my tip If you prefer a sweeter latte, add 1 tsp (5 mL) organic cane sugar to the freshly brewed espresso and stir until dissolved. Proceed with Step 1.

dalgona coffee

SERVES 2 · **5** 🍵 · TIME: 10 MINUTES

I learned how to make dalgona coffee, a popular Korean drink, during quarantine, when it became super popular on social media. It's extremely sweet, so I prefer not to have it first thing in the morning, even though it is coffee. You'll be astonished how only a few ingredients can make such a creamy, fluffy whip. It's the perfect recipe to make for you and a friend!

2 tbsp (30 mL) instant coffee granules
2 tbsp (30 mL) organic cane sugar
2 tbsp (30 mL) hot water
1 cup (250 mL) ice cubes

2 cups (500 mL) unsweetened nondairy milk

Electric mixer (see my tip)

1. Combine the instant coffee, sugar and hot water in a medium bowl. Using an electric mixer, beat at high speed for about 3 minutes. It will first get bubbly, then frothy, then turn light golden brown, and then it will form stiff peaks.

2. Divide the ice between two glasses. Add the nondairy milk, then top with dollops of the whipped coffee. Serve.

my tip You can whip the coffee with a whisk, but it will take close to 8 minutes and will definitely require some elbow grease!

mmmocha latte

SERVES 1 • 5 ⬤ • TIME: 10 MINUTES

A mocha latte combines two of my favorite things: coffee and chocolate. It was my gateway into coffee drinking because it's similar to hot chocolate, which I have always loved. During the holidays I make this latte extra fancy by adding a dollop of coconut whipped topping and some crushed candy cane on top.

1 cup (250 mL) freshly brewed coffee

1 tbsp (15 mL) unsweetened cocoa powder

1 tbsp (15 mL) organic cane sugar

½ cup (125 mL) unsweetened nondairy milk

1. Combine the coffee, cocoa and sugar in a small pot over high heat. Heat, whisking constantly, for about 1 minute, until the sugar is dissolved.

2. Pour the mixture into a mug, then return the pot to high heat. Add the nondairy milk; bring to a gentle simmer, whisking constantly, for about 1 minute, until the mixture is just starting to steam. Whisk vigorously for about 1 minute, until the mixture froths.

3. Gently pour the warm milk into the mug and spoon out froth overtop. Enjoy immediately.

my tip If you have a milk frother and prefer to use it instead of the stovetop method, complete Step 1, then use the frother as directed.

frothy vanilla latte

SERVES 1 • **5** ⬤ • TIME: 5 MINUTES

There aren't many days that a sweet, frothy vanilla latte can't make better. This used to be my coffee shop go-to, but now I pride myself on making an even better version at home — without needing an expensive espresso machine! This recipe uses a stovetop method to froth the milk, but if you have a milk frother, it will be even quicker to make (see my tips).

1 cup (250 mL) freshly brewed coffee
½ cup (125 mL) unsweetened nondairy milk

1 tbsp (15 mL) organic cane sugar
1 tsp (5 mL) vanilla extract (see my tips)

1. Pour the coffee into a mug. Set aside.

2. Combine the nondairy milk, sugar and vanilla in a small pot over high heat. Bring to a gentle simmer, whisking constantly for about 1 minute, until the sugar dissolves and the mixture is just starting to steam. Whisk vigorously for about 1 minute more, until the mixture froths.

3. Gently pour the warm milk mixture into the mug and spoon the froth overtop. Enjoy immediately.

my tips If you have a milk frother and prefer to use it instead of the stovetop method, complete Step 1. Then use the frother as directed.

Feel free to switch up the flavoring extract. Caramel and hazelnut work really well in this recipe.

breakfasts

one-bowl blueberry muffins

MAKES 12 MUFFINS • ● • TIME: 45 MINUTES

Blueberry muffins are my favorite type of muffin, hands down. These are super fast to whip up and taste incredible! I love to make them when I have some blueberries that are just a bit too squishy and on their way out. My suggestion: make a full batch of these and freeze half for the following week.

2 cups (500 mL) all-purpose flour
1 cup (250 mL) organic cane sugar
2 tsp (10 mL) baking powder
¼ tsp (1 mL) ground cinnamon
Pinch salt
1¼ cups (310 mL) unsweetened nondairy milk

⅓ cup (75 mL) vegan butter or coconut oil, melted
1 tsp (5 mL) vanilla extract
1¼ cups (310 mL) fresh or frozen blueberries (thawed if frozen)

12-cup muffin tin, greased or lined with paper liners

1. Preheat the oven to 350°F (180°C).

2. Whisk together the flour, sugar, baking powder, cinnamon and salt in a large bowl. Add the nondairy milk, vegan butter and vanilla; stir until just combined. The batter should be mostly smooth with a few lumps. Gently fold in the blueberries.

3. Spoon into the prepared muffin tin filling each cup about three-quarters full.

4. Bake in the preheated oven for 20 to 22 minutes or until a toothpick inserted in the center of a muffin comes out clean.

5. Remove from the oven and let cool in the muffin tin for 15 minutes, then transfer to a wire rack to cool completely. Store in an airtight container at room temperature for up to 3 days or in the freezer for up to 3 months.

my tip If you're more of a chocolate chip muffin person (no shame in that!), replace the blueberries with ¾ cup (175 mL) vegan chocolate chips.

pressure cooker apple cinnamon oatmeal

SERVES 4 • ⬤ • TIME: 25 MINUTES

One of my favorite fall activities is apple picking. Since we always leave with more apples than we know what to do with, this oatmeal recipe — which tastes like warm apple pie — really comes in handy. I love that you can throw everything in the pressure cooker first thing in the morning and, by the time you're finished getting ready for the day, breakfast is served!

2 cups (500 mL) peeled and diced firm apples, such as Granny Smith

2 cups (500 mL) large-flake (old-fashioned) rolled oats

¼ cup (60 mL) lightly packed brown sugar

4 cups (1 L) water

1½ cups (375 mL) unsweetened apple juice

2 tsp (10 mL) ground cinnamon

¼ tsp (1 mL) ground nutmeg

2 tbsp (30 mL) pure maple syrup (optional)

Electric pressure cooker

1. Combine the apples, oats, brown sugar, water, apple juice, cinnamon and nutmeg in the pressure cooker pot. Secure the lid and cook on high pressure for 6 minutes.

2. Once the cooking is finished, quick-release the pressure. Remove the lid and stir well. Let cool slightly before serving.

3. Divide among 4 bowls. Top with maple syrup (if using).

my tip This is a great Sunday meal-prep breakfast. Once the oatmeal has cooled, transfer to an airtight container and store in the fridge for up to 4 days. To reheat, place the oatmeal in a small pot over medium-low heat. Heat for 10 minutes, stirring frequently, until warmed through. Add 1 tbsp (15 mL) nondairy milk at a time, as needed, if it gets too thin.

light & fluffy pancakes

MAKES 6 PANCAKES (ABOUT 2 SERVINGS) • **5** • **TIME: 20 MINUTES**

Vegan pancakes are a tough recipe to perfect. Without eggs it's hard to get the fluffiness and lift everyone craves. However, using the right ratio of baking powder to flour, it is achievable! This is one of my most popular blog recipes — I get messages *every day* from people who made them and were so happy to find a vegan pancake recipe that turns out fluffy and delicious every time.

1 cup (250 mL) unsweetened nondairy milk
1 tbsp (15 mL) apple cider vinegar
1 cup (250 mL) all-purpose flour

2 tbsp (30 mL) organic cane sugar
2 tsp (10 mL) baking powder
Pinch salt
Vegetable oil

1. Combine the nondairy milk and apple cider vinegar in a small bowl. Set aside.

2. Whisk together the flour, sugar, baking powder and salt in a medium bowl.

3. Pour the milk mixture into the flour mixture and stir until just combined (a few lumps are okay).

4. Heat a large frying pan over medium heat. Add 1 tbsp (15 mL) vegetable oil and swirl it around the pan. Working in batches, spoon ¼ cup (60 mL) batter into the pan for each pancake (you should be able to cook 2 or 3 at a time). Cook for about 5 minutes, until bubbles rise to the surface and burst and the bottom is golden brown. Flip and cook for another 30 seconds to 1 minute on the other side, until the batter is set around the edges. Repeat with the remaining batter and vegetable oil.

5. Remove from the pan and serve immediately.

> my tip I love to serve these with vegan butter and maple syrup, but they're also great with a dollop of vegan chocolate hazelnut spread and some sliced banana.

best-ever weekend waffles

MAKES 4 WAFFLES (ABOUT 4 SERVINGS) • ⬤ • TIME: 30 MINUTES

If you're looking for a no-fail vegan waffle recipe that's sure to impress, this one is for you. It's adapted from an older recipe on my blog, but this one replaces puréed pumpkin with applesauce, which is easier to find year round. My friends Katie and Brock make these waffles every Saturday and claim they're the best waffles they've ever had! If you want to jazz them up for a special brunch, top them with fresh fruit and coconut whipped cream.

1½ cups (375 mL) all-purpose flour
2 tbsp (30 mL) organic cane sugar
1 tbsp (15 mL) baking powder
1 tsp (5 mL) ground cinnamon
1½ cups (375 mL) unsweetened nondairy milk

2 tbsp (30 mL) unsweetened applesauce
1 tbsp (15 mL) vegetable oil
2 tsp (10 mL) white vinegar
Cooking spray or melted vegan butter

Waffle iron
Rimmed baking sheet

1. Preheat the oven to 200°F (100°C).

2. Whisk together the flour, sugar, baking powder and cinnamon in a large bowl.

3. Add the nondairy milk, applesauce, vegetable oil and vinegar; stir until just combined. Do not overmix — the batter will have small lumps, and that's okay!

4. Preheat the waffle iron.

5. Grease the waffle iron with cooking spray or vegan butter. Working in batches, spread about ½ cup (125 mL) batter evenly onto the prepared waffle iron. Close the lid and cook for about 5 minutes or until golden and crispy. Transfer the waffle to the baking sheet and keep warm in the preheated oven.

6. Repeat with the remaining batter, greasing the waffle iron lightly in between batches. Serve.

my tip These waffles are great with vegan butter and maple syrup but extra tasty piled high with toppings like berries, banana and coconut whipped cream.

sheet-pan western-ish omelet

SERVES 4 TO 6 • ◆ • **TIME: 30 MINUTES**

Before going vegan, I loved having an omelet for breakfast almost every day. So, understandably, once I stopped eating eggs, I had to quickly find a replacement that would satisfy my love for this breakfast dish. This Western-inspired omelet is super easy to make and goes well with hash browns and toast. It's also great layered on a bagel like a breakfast sandwich. My favorite!

1¼ cups (310 mL) chickpea flour

2 tbsp (30 mL) nutritional yeast

1 tsp (5 mL) baking powder

¼ tsp (1 mL) garlic powder

½ tsp (2 mL) salt

1¼ cups (310 mL) water

½ cup (125 mL) finely chopped red onion

½ cup (125 mL) finely chopped bell pepper

½ cup (125 mL) chopped vegan sausage or vegan ham (optional)

1 cup (250 mL) shredded vegan Cheddar cheese (optional)

¼ tsp (1 mL) black pepper

13- by 9-inch (33 by 23 cm) rimmed baking sheet, lined with parchment paper

1. Preheat the oven to 375°F (190°C).

2. Whisk together the chickpea flour, nutritional yeast, baking powder, garlic powder and salt in a large bowl. Add the water; whisk to combine.

3. Pour the chickpea mixture onto the prepared baking sheet and spread in a thin layer using the back of a spoon. Evenly sprinkle with the red onion, bell pepper, vegan sausage (if using), vegan Cheddar cheese (if using) and black pepper.

4. Bake in the preheated oven for 10 to 12 minutes, until set and golden with a few cracks on top.

5. Remove from the oven and let cool on the baking sheet for 10 minutes, then slice and serve. Store any leftovers in an airtight container in the fridge for up to 4 days. See my tip for freezing instructions.

my tip The cooked omelet freezes and reheats well. Once it's cooled, slice and layer it in a freezer-safe container, with pieces of parchment paper between the slices to prevent sticking. To reheat, place the frozen slices on a baking sheet; bake in an oven preheated to 350°F (180°C) for about 10 minutes or until heated through. Or you can reheat them in a frying pan with a lid over medium heat for 10 minutes or until heated through.

fabulous french toast

SERVES 4 • **5** • TIME: 50 MINUTES

I was always disappointed with past trials of vegan French toast. Most of the versions I tried were slightly mushy and sad. Thankfully, I've found a winning combination that results in perfect French toast, without the dreaded soggy center. The key ingredient is tofu, which, when blended, adds an eggy texture that creates an incredible golden and crispy exterior.

1 cup (250 mL) vanilla nondairy milk
6 oz (175 g) firm tofu, coarsely chopped
1 tsp (5 mL) ground cinnamon
¼ cup (60 mL) vegan butter, divided

8 thick bread slices, such as sourdough or Italian

Blender
Large rimmed baking sheet

1. Preheat the oven to 200°F (100°C).

2. Place the nondairy milk, tofu and cinnamon in a blender. Blend on high speed for about 30 seconds, until smooth. Pour the mixture into a shallow bowl.

3. Heat a large frying pan over medium heat. Add 1 tbsp (15 mL) vegan butter to the pan. Once it's sizzling, dip a slice of bread into the tofu mixture, allowing any excess batter to drip off. Place in the pan (you should be able to fit in 2 pieces at once). Cook for about 5 minutes per side or until crispy and golden brown. Place the cooked French toast on a baking sheet and keep warm in the preheated oven.

4. Repeat with the remaining butter, bread and tofu mixture. Discard excess tofu mixture. Serve.

my tip I love to serve this with maple syrup, a sprinkle of confectioners' (icing) sugar and some fresh berries.

frying pan maple granola

I love granola. Making it, eating it — I can't get enough. I wanted to see if I could find a way to make it even quicker for those summer mornings when you get a craving but don't want to turn on the oven. Enter frying pan granola made in a single frying pan in 15 minutes. Breakfast goals!

2 tbsp (30 mL) coconut oil

1 cup (250 mL) large-flake (old-fashioned) rolled oats

½ cup (125 mL) salted roasted almonds

½ cup (125 mL) sunflower seeds

¼ cup (60 mL) pure maple syrup

½ tsp (2 mL) ground cinnamon

1. Melt the coconut oil in a large frying pan over medium heat. Add the oats, almonds, sunflower seeds, maple syrup and cinnamon; stir to combine. Cook, stirring frequently, for about 10 minutes or until golden brown and fragrant.

2. Remove from the heat and let cool completely in the pan. The granola will be slightly chewy when still warm, but it will crisp up perfectly as it cools. Serve or store in an airtight container or jar at room temperature for 1 week or in the fridge for up to 2 weeks.

my tip I love sprinkling this granola over a bowl of coconut yogurt with fresh berries. It also makes an amazing crunchy topping for vegan ice cream and smoothie bowls.

tomato chickpeas on toast

SERVES 4 • ⬤ • TIME: 35 MINUTES

There is a hashtag on Instagram called #stuffontoast that I love browsing for inspiration. After seeing so many photos of beans on toast I decided to try my hand at creating one of my own! These chickpeas are simmered in a luscious tomato base and served on top of sourdough toast. It's a great recipe as part of a brunch spread, because you can prep everything ahead of time. All you'll have to do is toast the bread.

1 tbsp (15 mL) vegetable oil

½ onion, thinly sliced

1 can (14 oz/398 mL) chickpeas, drained and rinsed

1 tsp (5 mL) smoked paprika (see my tip)

1 tsp (5 mL) ground cumin

½ tsp (2 mL) salt

½ tsp (2 mL) black pepper

¼ tsp (1 mL) garlic powder

⅛ tsp (0.5 mL) ground cinnamon

1 can (28 oz/796 mL) no-salt-added diced tomatoes (with juice)

4 slices sourdough bread, toasted

1. Heat the vegetable oil in a large frying pan over medium heat. Add the onion and cook for about 5 minutes, until translucent.

2. Add the chickpeas, smoked paprika, cumin, salt, pepper, garlic powder and cinnamon; stir to coat. Using a potato masher or the back of a spoon, lightly mash the chickpeas. Add the tomatoes (with juice); stir to combine. Lower the heat to medium-low and simmer for about 20 minutes, stirring occasionally, until thickened slightly.

3. Remove from the heat and let cool slightly. Divide the chickpea mixture evenly on top of toast slices; serve.

my tip Smoked paprika is easy to find in the spice aisle of most well-stocked grocery stores. You can also often find it in bulk food stores, which is great if you want to buy only a small amount. However, if you have only regular paprika, don't sweat it! You can substitute the same amount of regular paprika for the smoked.

bridget's tofu breakfast

SERVES 4 • **5** • TIME: 25 MINUTES

This recipe was created by my sister Bridget when she didn't have all the ingredients to make a tofu scramble recipe she'd found on Pinterest. Using only what she had in her fridge, she improvised this recipe, which became our favorite quick breakfast. It seems too easy to taste good, but I can assure you it does. I love to serve this with a toasted slice of my Classic White Sandwich Bread (page 177).

12 oz (375 g) firm tofu, pressed (see my tips)
1 tbsp (15 mL) vegetable oil
½ red onion, finely chopped

½ red bell pepper, finely chopped
1 tbsp (15 mL) hot sauce
Salt and black pepper

1. Heat the vegetable oil in a large frying pan over medium heat. Crumble the tofu into the pan and cook for about 5 minutes, stirring frequently, until starting to brown. Add the onion and red pepper; cook for about 5 minutes, stirring frequently, until the onion softens slightly.

2. Add the hot sauce and a sprinkle of salt and pepper; stir to combine. Cook for about 3 minutes more, stirring frequently, until the tofu is golden.

3. Remove from the heat and serve.

my tips Place the tofu on a clean, folded dish towel. Place another folded dish towel on top, followed by a large pot or frying pan. Let stand for 5 to 10 minutes while the towels absorb the moisture.

Store any leftovers in an airtight container in the fridge for up to 3 days. Reheat in a large frying pan with 1 tsp (5 mL) vegetable oil over medium-low heat for about 10 minutes, stirring occasionally, until warm. Alternatively, microwave in a microwave-safe bowl on High for about 2 minutes or until warm.

smoky tofu & hash brown bake

SERVES 4 • ◆ • TIME: 1 HOUR

When I'm in the mood for a big breakfast, I usually go for something savory, and this fits the bill! This recipe was inspired by a diner breakfast I had many years ago. I remember seeing that piping-hot skillet of smoky potatoes and scrambled eggs and thinking that I could eat it every day. Now I opt for this version, which uses tofu instead of eggs, and it always hits the spot when I wake up extra-hungry.

Roasted Potatoes
4 cups (1 L) diced russet potatoes (about 4 medium)
1 tbsp (15 mL) vegetable oil
1 tsp (5 mL) salt
¼ tsp (1 mL) black pepper

Smoky BBQ Tofu
2 tbsp (30 mL) brown sugar
2 tbsp (30 mL) vegetable oil
2 tbsp (30 mL) ketchup
2 tbsp (30 mL) reduced-sodium soy sauce

1 tsp (5 mL) liquid smoke
¼ tsp (1 mL) onion powder
¼ tsp (1 mL) garlic powder
12 oz (375 g) firm tofu, crumbled
½ onion, sliced

Optional Toppings
1 ripe avocado, diced
1 green onion, sliced

Large rimmed baking sheet, lined with parchment paper

1. Preheat the oven to 400°F (200°C).

2. **ROASTED POTATOES** Place the potatoes in a large bowl. Add the vegetable oil, salt and pepper; stir to coat. Spread onto the prepared baking sheet (reserve the bowl), leaving one-third of the space free for the tofu. Bake in the preheated oven for 20 minutes.

3. **SMOKY BBQ TOFU** Meanwhile, add the brown sugar, vegetable oil, ketchup, soy sauce, liquid smoke, onion powder and garlic powder to the reserved bowl; stir to combine. Add the tofu and onion; stir to coat.

4. Remove the baking sheet from the oven. Spread the tofu over the reserved space on the sheet. Bake for about 20 minutes more, until the potatoes are fork-tender and the tofu is starting to brown.

5. Remove from the oven and let cool slightly before serving. Divide among 4 bowls and top with diced avocado and green onion slices (if using). Serve.

chorizo tempeh breakfast wraps

SERVES 4 • ◈ • TIME: 35 MINUTES

These wraps are hearty and super filling. The tempeh is seasoned with chili powder, cumin and garlic to give it a spicy, smoky flavor similar to chorizo sausage. And for my on-the-go breakfast crew, the wraps are super easy to make ahead of time (see my tip).

1½ cups (375 mL) peeled and cubed sweet potato (about 1 small)

½ onion, sliced

2 tbsp (30 mL) vegetable oil, divided

½ tsp (2 mL) salt

12 oz (375 g) tempeh, roughly chopped

1 red bell pepper, sliced

1 tbsp (15 mL) nutritional yeast

1 tsp (5 mL) chili powder

1 tsp (5 mL) ground cumin

¼ tsp (1 mL) garlic powder

2 cups (500 mL) coarsely chopped kale, ribs removed

4 flour tortillas

½ cup (125 mL) tomato salsa

Large rimmed baking sheet, lined with parchment paper

1. Preheat the oven to 400°F (200°C).

2. Place the sweet potato, onion, 1 tbsp (15 mL) oil and salt in a large bowl; toss to coat. Spread onto the prepared baking sheet in an even layer (reserve the bowl) and bake in the preheated oven for 10 minutes or until the onion is starting to brown.

3. Meanwhile, add the tempeh, bell pepper, remaining 1 tbsp (15 mL) oil, nutritional yeast, chili powder, cumin and garlic powder to the reserved bowl; toss to coat. Add to the baking sheet and stir gently to combine. Bake for about 15 minutes, until the sweet potato is fork-tender and the tempeh is golden. Remove from the oven, add the kale and bake for 2 more minutes, until the kale is slightly wilted.

4. Remove from the oven. Divide the mixture among the tortillas and top evenly with salsa. Roll each tortilla up from the bottom, like a burrito. Serve.

my tip These wraps are great to make ahead, but the directions differ slightly from the recipe. After reheating, serve with salsa on the side for dipping. **TO FREEZE** Let the filling cool completely. Assemble through Step 4, but do not add salsa. Wrap tightly in plastic wrap and store in the freezer for up to 3 months. **TO REHEAT FROM FROZEN IN THE MICROWAVE** Remove plastic, then wrap tortilla in a damp paper towel. Place on a plate and microwave on High for 2 to 3 minutes, until heated through. **TO REHEAT FROM FROZEN IN THE OVEN** Preheat the oven to 375°F (190°C). Remove plastic and place tortilla on a baking sheet. Bake in the oven for 20 minutes or until heated through.

snacks
& apps

liv's popcorn chick'n

SERVES 4 · **5** · TIME: 1 HOUR

As a vegan, I can't eat at most fast-food chains, so this recipe really comes in handy when I get a craving! These bites are crispy, meaty and perfect for dipping in ketchup or plum sauce. The trick is to use a vegan chicken-flavored broth (I buy it at my bulk store, but you can also find vegan chicken stock cubes online).

1 cup (250 mL) vital wheat gluten

2 tbsp (30 mL) chickpea flour
(see my tips)

4 cups (1 L) vegan chicken broth, divided

½ cup (125 mL) all-purpose flour

Pinch salt and black pepper

3 tbsp (45 mL) coconut oil

Electric pressure cooker

1. Whisk together the vital wheat gluten and chickpea flour in a large bowl.

2. Add 1 cup (250 mL) vegan chicken broth and stir until a dough forms. Using your hands, knead the dough a few times in the bowl until there are no dry spots. You've made seitan!

3. Add 3 cups (750 mL) broth to the pressure cooker pot. Rip the seitan into bite-size chunks and add to the pot. Secure the lid and cook on high pressure for 15 minutes.

4. Meanwhile, whisk together the all-purpose flour, salt and pepper. Set aside.

5. Once the seitan has finished cooking, quick-release the pressure. Drain the broth and add the seitan pieces to the flour mixture. Toss to coat.

6. Melt the coconut oil in a large frying pan over medium heat. Once the oil is shimmering, add the seitan and cook for about 5 minutes per side, until crispy and golden brown all over. Transfer to a large bowl lined with paper towels. Let cool slightly before serving.

my tips If you can't find chickpea flour, you can substitute 2 tbsp (30 mL) nutritional yeast instead. The flavor won't change — I make it both ways frequently!

Store leftovers in an airtight container in the fridge for up to 5 days or in the freezer for up to 3 months. **TO REHEAT FROM THE FRIDGE** Place in a large frying pan over medium heat. Heat for about 10 minutes, stirring frequently, until crispy and warmed. **TO REHEAT FROM FROZEN** Preheat the oven to 350°F (180°C) and bake on a rimmed baking sheet for 20 minutes, flipping the pieces halfway through, until golden and warm.

cheesy salsa baked dip

MAKES APPROX. 3 CUPS (750 ML) • **5** • TIME: 45 MINUTES

This dip recipe was inspired by chile con queso, a dish made with melted cheese and chili peppers. It has been my star dish for so many gatherings — Superbowl parties, Christmas Eve, Saturday nights at home with friends — you name it. I like to serve it with a heaping bowl of tortilla chips for dipping. You can really change up the flavor by using different types of salsa. For example, if you're a spice lover, definitely choose a hot salsa!

2 cups (500 mL) peeled and diced white potatoes (about 1½ medium)

½ cup (125 mL) chopped carrot (about 1 large)

¼ cup (60 mL) raw cashews

¼ cup (60 mL) nutritional yeast

Pinch salt

Water

1 jar (15 oz/425 mL) chunky tomato salsa

High-powered blender or food processor
6-cup (1.5 L) casserole dish

1. Preheat the oven to 425°F (220°C).

2. Place the potatoes and carrot in a large pot and add enough water to cover by 2 inches (5 cm); bring to a boil over high heat. Add the cashews and reduce the heat to medium-low. Boil gently for about 10 minutes, until softened. Drain and rinse under cold water until cooled completely.

3. Add the cooked potatoes, carrot and cashews, nutritional yeast, salt and ¾ cup (175 mL) water to a high-powered blender; blend on high speed for about 2 minutes, until smooth. Pour into the casserole dish and add the salsa; stir to combine.

4. Bake in the preheated oven for about 15 minutes or until heated through and the top is set and cracked slightly. Remove from the oven and let cool slightly before serving.

bruschetta pizza

MAKES 32 BITES • ⬥ • TIME: 45 MINUTES
(PLUS 30 MINUTES FOR RISING)

Most of the time when I see bruschetta on the menu at a restaurant, I can't pass it up — the combination of tomatoes, garlic and fresh basil is just irresistible! I decided to put a little twist on this Italian app by making it in pizza form. This pizza is great whole if you want to eat it as a main, but when serving it as an app, I like to slice it into bite-size pieces and skewer them with toothpicks.

Pizza Dough
1 cup (250 mL) warm water
1 tsp (5 mL) quick-rising (instant) yeast
1 tsp (5 mL) organic cane sugar
2 cups (500 mL) all-purpose flour (approx.)
Vegetable oil
Pinch salt

Bruschetta Topping
2 cups (500 mL) diced fresh plum (Roma) tomatoes (about 3)
½ white onion, diced

3 garlic cloves, minced
¼ cup (60 mL) packed fresh basil leaves
2 tbsp (30 mL) olive oil
1 cup (250 mL) store-bought pizza sauce (see my tip)
1½ cups (375 mL) vegan mozzarella cheese shreds
Salt and black pepper

13- by 9-inch (33 by 23 cm) rimmed baking sheet, lined with parchment paper

Toothpicks (optional)

1. **PIZZA DOUGH** Place the water, yeast and sugar in a large bowl; stir gently until just combined. Let stand for 5 minutes, until bubbling slightly.

2. Add the flour, 1 tbsp (15 mL) vegetable oil and salt; stir to form a soft dough ball. Remove the dough from the bowl, reserving bowl, and knead 5 to 6 times on a lightly floured surface, until smooth.

3. Wash and dry the reserved bowl, then lightly grease with vegetable oil. Place the dough in the bowl and cover with a clean dish towel. Set aside in a warm, draft-free environment for 30 minutes, until the dough has doubled in size.

4. Meanwhile, preheat the oven to 425°F (220°C).

5. **BRUSCHETTA TOPPING** Combine the tomatoes, onion, garlic, basil and olive oil in a medium bowl. Set aside ½ cup (125 mL) of the mixture for when the pizza comes out of the oven.

6. Using your fingers, gently spread out the pizza dough on the prepared baking sheet in an even layer. Top with the pizza sauce, tomato mixture and vegan mozzarella cheese, leaving a 1-inch (2.5 cm) border. Bake in the preheated oven for 15 minutes or until the bottom of the crust is golden brown and the cheese is melted.

7. Remove from the oven and let cool slightly. Top with the reserved bruschetta mixture. Sprinkle with salt and pepper. Slice into 4 strips lengthwise and 8 strips widthwise to make 32 bites. Pierce the pieces with a toothpick (if using); serve.

my tip Most store-bought pizza sauces are vegan, but make sure to read the ingredients list before purchasing.

sweet potato & white bean bites

MAKES ABOUT 10 BITES • 5 • TIME: 35 MINUTES

These little patties are packed with flavor and perfect for dipping! I love to serve them with spicy mayo, which you can easily make by mixing together some vegan mayo and your favorite hot sauce. Serve these to friends or treat yourself. If you have leftovers, you can easily store them in the fridge and reheat in a frying pan (see my tips).

1 cup (250 mL) peeled and cubed sweet potato

1 cup (250 mL) cooked white beans, such as cannellini, drained and rinsed

½ cup (125 mL) all-purpose flour, divided

¼ cup (60 mL) finely chopped onion

Pinch salt

2 tbsp (30 mL) vegetable oil

Large rimmed baking sheet

1. Place the sweet potato in a medium pot and add enough water to cover by 2 inches (5 cm); bring to a boil over high heat. Cook for about 8 minutes, until fork-tender. Drain and return to the pot. Using a potato masher or fork, mash until smooth. Set aside to cool completely.

2. Place the beans in a large bowl. Using a potato masher or fork, mash them slightly. Add the mashed sweet potato, ¼ cup (60 mL) flour, onion and salt; stir to combine.

3. Place the remaining flour in a shallow bowl. With wet hands, form small patties out of the sweet potato mixture, about 2 tbsp (30 mL) each. Dip each patty in the flour, turning to ensure that all sides get coated, then set aside. Discard excess flour.

4. Heat the vegetable oil in a large frying pan over medium heat. Working in batches, add the patties to the pan and cook for about 6 minutes per side, until golden brown. Reduce the heat slightly if you notice any burning.

5. When they are cooked, transfer the patties to a serving plate; serve.

my tips Feel free to substitute 1 cup (250 mL) peeled and cubed white potato, turnip or carrot for the sweet potato.

Store leftovers in an airtight container in the fridge for up to 5 days. To reheat, add 1 tbsp (15 mL) vegetable oil to a frying pan over medium heat and cook for about 5 minutes per side, until warm.

baked almond feta

SERVES 4 TO 6 • **5** • TIME: 40 MINUTES

This recipe is one of my go-to apps for parties. You can whip it up ahead of time and then pop it in the oven just before people come over (see my tip). It's great served alongside crackers or tortilla chips or spread on toast. If I somehow manage to have any left over, I add it to salads or pasta. It might seem weird to make faux feta out of almonds, but almond flour has a mild flavor and, when mixed with other ingredients, the perfect texture to create this crumbly variety of cheese.

1½ cups (375 mL) almond flour

⅓ cup (75 mL) water

2 tbsp (30 mL) freshly squeezed lemon juice

1 tbsp (15 mL) nutritional yeast

1 garlic clove

½ tsp (2 mL) salt

Food processor or high-powered blender

12-inch (30 cm) square of double-thickness cheesecloth or a nut milk bag

Minimum 6-cup (1.5 L) casserole dish, lined with parchment paper

1. Preheat the oven to 350°F (180°C).

2. Combine the almond flour, water, lemon juice, nutritional yeast, garlic and salt in a food processor. Process for about 3 minutes, until smooth and creamy.

3. Place the almond mixture in the center of the cheesecloth or nut milk bag. Pull up the sides of the cheesecloth so the mixture forms a ball, and twist the top of the cheesecloth to squeeze it tightly. Open up the cheesecloth and flip it inside out, so the ball goes into the prepared baking dish. Flatten it slightly with the palm of your hand to form a disk.

4. Bake in the preheated oven for 30 minutes or until golden brown with a few cracks on top. Remove from the oven and let cool slightly before serving. Store leftovers in an airtight container in the fridge for up to 4 days.

my tip To add some extra oomph to this recipe, pour a drizzle of chili oil overtop, right before serving.

crispy garlic parm cauliflower wings

SERVES 4 • ⬭ • TIME: 45 MINUTES

These cauliflower "wings" are a hit in my house! They're crispy, coated in vegan Parmesan cheese and baked until golden brown. You can serve these with a variety of dipping sauces — my favorites include sweet Thai chili sauce, plum sauce and Spiced Tahini Sauce (page 22) — as well as using them to top a salad that needs an extra bit of heartiness.

1 cup (250 mL) all-purpose flour, divided

½ cup (125 mL) unsweetened nondairy milk

1 cup (250 mL) panko bread crumbs

⅓ cup (75 mL) vegan Parmesan cheese or Herb & Garlic Parmesan Sprinkle (page 27; see my tip)

1 tsp (5 mL) dried parsley

1 tsp (5 mL) salt

½ tsp (2 mL) garlic powder

1 medium cauliflower head, chopped into florets

Cooking spray

Large rimmed baking sheet, lined with parchment paper

1. Preheat the oven to 425°F (220°C).

2. Whisk together ½ cup (125 mL) flour and the nondairy milk in a large bowl, until smooth. Set aside.

3. Combine the panko crumbs, remaining ½ cup (125 mL) flour, vegan Parmesan cheese, parsley, salt and garlic powder in a separate large bowl.

4. Submerge a few cauliflower florets in the nondairy milk mixture until coated, shaking off any excess. Place in the crumb mixture; toss to coat. Arrange on the prepared baking sheet. Repeat with the remaining cauliflower.

5. Lightly spray the coated cauliflower with cooking spray. This will make the cauliflower pieces perfectly golden and crispy.

6. Bake in the preheated oven for 15 minutes. Flip and bake about 10 minutes more, until golden brown.

7. Remove from the oven and let cool slightly before serving.

my tip If using the Herb & Garlic Parmesan Sprinkle (page 27), omit the garlic powder.

pretzel bites

MAKES ABOUT 50 BITES • **5** • TIME: 50 MINUTES

When I was a preteen, my go-to snack at the mall was always pretzel bites. I couldn't resist the aroma of fresh dough wafting out of the pretzel shop as we walked past. This recipe makes a lot and they're best served fresh, so feel free to use half a ball of pizza dough and freeze the rest for another time (see my tip). If you're wondering about the baking soda step, it's necessary to get that authentic golden brown pretzel look and taste!

1 ball (1 lb/500 g) store-bought vegan pizza dough or 1 recipe Pizza Dough (page 84)

All-purpose flour for dusting

Water

⅓ cup (75 mL) baking soda

¼ cup (60 mL) vegan butter, melted

Coarse salt

1 recipe Crowd-Pleasing Beer & Cheese Dip (opposite), optional

Large rimmed baking sheet, lined with parchment paper

1. Preheat the oven to 375°F (190°C).

2. Divide the vegan pizza dough into 6 chunks. On a lightly floured surface, roll each chunk into a rope 1 inch (2.5 cm) thick. Slice each rope into 1-inch (2.5 cm) pieces.

3. Add 6 cups (1.5 L) water to a large pot and bring to a boil. Slowly add the baking soda; stir to combine.

4. Using a slotted spoon or mesh strainer, lower 5 pieces of dough into the boiling water. Cook for about 15 seconds, until slightly firm. Using the slotted spoon or strainer, remove the bites, allowing excess water to drip off, and place on the prepared baking sheet. Repeat with the remaining dough.

5. Lightly brush the tops with melted vegan butter and sprinkle each piece with salt.

6. Bake in the preheated oven for about 12 minutes, until brown on top. Remove from the oven and let cool slightly on the baking sheet, then transfer to a serving dish. Serve with Crowd-Pleasing Beer & Cheese Dip (if using) for the ultimate pretzel experience.

my tip Store leftovers in an airtight container in the fridge for up to 5 days. To reheat, add 1 tbsp (15 mL) vegetable oil to a frying pan over medium heat and cook for about 5 minutes per side, until warm.

crowd-pleasing
beer & cheese dip

MAKES 1½ CUPS (175 ML) • ⬤ • TIME: 15 MINUTES

I created this dip to serve with my Pretzel Bites (opposite), but it's also great for game-day parties when served in a bread bowl (see my tips). I've included an option for those who wish to make this without the beer, which I've explained how to do below.

3 tbsp (45 mL) vegan butter

3 tbsp (45 mL) all-purpose flour

⅓ cup (75 mL) beer (see my tips)

½ cup (125 mL) unsweetened nondairy milk

1 tsp (5 mL) Dijon mustard

2 cups (500 mL) shredded vegan Cheddar cheese

Salt and black pepper

1. Melt the vegan butter in a medium pot over medium heat. Add the flour and whisk to combine. Immediately add the beer and bring to a simmer, whisking constantly, for about 3 minutes, until the sauce has thickened.

2. Add the nondairy milk and Dijon mustard; whisk until combined. Add the vegan Cheddar cheese; stir until melted and smooth. Add salt and pepper to taste. Serve immediately.

my tips **CHOOSING A BEER FOR THIS RECIPE** The dip tastes like whatever beer you use, so use a type you like. I suggest a lager amber or pale ale. Avoid fruity, sour or very hoppy beers. If you do not wish to use beer in this recipe, substitute ⅓ cup (75 mL) unsweetened nondairy milk plus 1 tbsp (15 mL) freshly squeezed lemon juice instead (you'll use ¾ cup + 5 tsp/200 mL unsweetened nondairy milk total). The flavor will be less bitter, more like a regular cheese sauce. **BREAD BOWL** Purchase a small, round loaf of bread with a crusty exterior. Sourdough, rye or Italian bread works well. Cut a thin slice off the top of the loaf. Using your hands, rip out chunks to hollow out the inside, leaving an outer shell roughly ½ inch (1 cm) thick. Use the bread chunks to dip, or save them to make croutons!

buffalo chickpea nachos

SERVES 4 • ⬤ • TIME: 30 MINUTES

Up your nachos game with this version that uses spicy Buffalo chickpeas. The chickpeas are cooked in my Vegan Buffalo Sauce (page 26), then spread over the nachos and layered with bell pepper and melty vegan cheese, and garnished with crisp green onions. I love to add Super-Quick Fresh Tomato Salsa (page 21) and guacamole if I have time to make them.

1 can (14 oz/398 mL) chickpeas, drained and rinsed

1 recipe Vegan Buffalo Sauce (page 26; see my tip)

¼ tsp (1 mL) black pepper

1 bag (10 oz/295 g) tortilla chips

2 cups (500 mL) shredded vegan Cheddar cheese

1 red bell pepper, chopped

¼ cup (60 mL) chopped green onions

Large rimmed baking sheet

1. Preheat the oven to 375°F (190°C).

2. Combine the chickpeas, vegan Buffalo sauce and black pepper in a medium bowl; stir to coat. Using a potato masher or fork, mash the chickpeas slightly. Set aside.

3. Spread the tortilla chips on the baking sheet in an even layer. Sprinkle the vegan Cheddar cheese overtop. Add the chickpea mixture in an even layer, followed by the bell pepper.

4. Bake in the preheated oven for about 10 minutes, until the cheese is melted and the chips are starting to turn golden around the edges. Watch the nachos so they don't burn!

5. Remove from the oven and let cool slightly. Top with green onion; serve.

my tip You can save time by making a batch of Vegan Buffalo Sauce ahead of time. It keeps well in the fridge for up to 1 week.

maple nut hempies

MAKES 12 BALLS • **5** 🔻 • TIME: 10 MINUTES

These balls take 10 minutes to whip up and are just the right size to pack in a lunch box. Made with all the good stuff — nut butter, maple syrup, hemp seeds, oats and vanilla — they can satisfy a sweet tooth while keeping your energy up. I always try to have a batch in my fridge so I can grab one after a workout!

¼ cup (60 mL) creamy natural nut butter (see my tip)

3 tbsp (45 mL) pure maple syrup

1 tsp (5 mL) vanilla extract

Pinch salt

½ cup (125 mL) large-flake (old-fashioned) rolled oats

2 tbsp (30 mL) hemp seeds

1. Combine the nut butter, maple syrup, vanilla and salt in a medium bowl. Stir in the oats and hemp seeds until well combined.

2. Using your hands, form the mixture into balls, using 1½ tbsp (22 mL) for each. Serve immediately or store in an airtight container in the fridge for up to 1 week or in the freezer for up to 1 month.

my tip A creamy natural nut butter (meaning the only ingredient is nuts) is best for this recipe. Feel free to use whatever nut or seed butter you like best. I prefer almond butter, but cashew, peanut or sunflower seed butter will be great too.

no-bake chocolate almond oat bars

MAKES 12 BARS • 5 • TIME: 15 MINUTES
(PLUS 1 HOUR FOR CHILLING)

A similar, non-vegan version of this recipe was sent to me by my grandma Joan, with a note about how she thought I could easily make it vegan. I immediately wanted to try out these bars, so I made a few swaps — maple syrup instead of honey, vegan chocolate for the milk chocolate — and they're delicious!

½ cup (125 mL) crunchy almond butter
½ cup (125 mL) pure maple syrup
½ cup (125 mL) coconut oil
¾ cup (175 mL) vegan chocolate chips

2 cups (500 mL) large-flake
(old-fashioned) rolled oats

**9-inch (23 cm) square metal pan,
greased or lined with parchment paper**

1. Combine the almond butter, maple syrup and coconut oil in a large pot over medium heat. Cook for about 3 minutes, stirring constantly, until the oil is melted and the mixture is well combined.

2. Add the vegan chocolate chips and stir constantly until melted. Add the oats and stir until coated.

3. Press the mixture into the prepared baking pan and refrigerate for at least 1 hour. Transfer to the counter and let come to room temperature for 10 minutes. Slice into 12 bars. Serve or store in an airtight container in the fridge for up to 5 days or in the freezer for up to 2 weeks.

my tip If you are a peanut-butter lover, feel free to substitute ½ cup (125 mL) crunchy peanut butter for the almond butter.

soups
& salads

spicy vegan italian sausage & kale soup

SERVES 4 • ● • TIME: 30 MINUTES

This spicy soup is brothy yet filling, and perfect for a crisp fall evening when you want to warm up. I love adding sturdy greens here because it really complements the richness of the sausage. I typically use a short pasta for this recipe; rotini, penne and macaroni are all great options.

2 tbsp (30 mL) olive oil
2 vegan Italian sausages, crumbled
1 large carrot, thinly sliced into rounds
½ onion, finely chopped
2 garlic cloves, minced
1 tsp (5 mL) dried Italian seasoning
½ tsp (2 mL) hot pepper flakes

Salt and black pepper
4 cups (1 L) low-sodium vegetable broth
2 cups (500 mL) water
1¼ cups (310 mL) rotini, penne or other short pasta
2 cups (500 mL) finely chopped kale, ribs removed

1. Heat the olive oil in a large pot over medium heat. Add the vegan sausage, carrot, onion and garlic; cook for 5 minutes, stirring frequently, until the onion is translucent and the carrot have softened slightly.

2. Add the Italian seasoning, hot pepper flakes and a sprinkle of salt and pepper; stir to coat. Add the broth, water and pasta. Increase the heat to high and bring to a boil. Reduce the heat to medium-low and simmer for about 8 minutes, stirring occasionally, until the pasta is cooked.

3. Add the kale and cook for about 1 minute, stirring occasionally, until wilted. Serve.

my tip This soup doesn't keep well, because the pasta will eventually absorb the liquid and become mushy. I like to make it when I know it will all get eaten on the first day, or I make half a batch.

white lasagna soup

SERVES 4 • 🍵 • TIME: 40 MINUTES

When I was growing up, I loved lasagna night with my cousins. But my younger cousin Kate wasn't able to eat tomato products, so my uncle always made a white lasagna with béchamel sauce for her. I still think about it to this day, and that's what inspired this tomato-free alternative to my famous lasagna soup recipe (which you can find in my first cookbook).

2 tbsp (30 mL) olive oil
1 large carrot, finely chopped
½ large onion, finely chopped
2 large garlic cloves, minced
2 tbsp (30 mL) all-purpose flour
4 cups (1 L) low-sodium vegetable broth
2 cans (each 14 oz/398 mL) full-fat coconut milk

3½ cups (875 mL) mini lasagna noodles, or 8 lasagna noodles broken into pieces
1 tsp (5 mL) dried sage
½ tsp (2 mL) dried oregano
Salt and black pepper
1 cup (250 mL) vegan mozzarella cheese shreds
2 cups (500 mL) packed baby spinach

1. Heat the olive oil in a large pot over medium heat. Add the carrot, onion and garlic; cook for about 5 minutes, stirring occasionally, until the carrot has softened slightly.

2. Sprinkle in the flour; stir to coat. Add ¼ cup (60 mL) broth; stir to combine. Continue adding broth about ¼ cup (60 mL) at a time, stirring constantly, until sauce has thickened slightly, about 8 minutes in total.

3. Add the coconut milk, lasagna noodles, sage, oregano and a sprinkle of salt and pepper; stir to combine. Increase the heat to high and bring to a boil. Reduce the heat to medium-low, cover and simmer gently for about 15 minutes, until the noodles are tender.

4. Add the vegan mozzarella cheese and stir constantly for 2 minutes, until melted. Add the spinach and stir constantly for about 1 minute, until wilted. Taste and add additional salt and pepper if desired; serve.

apple, squash & cheddar soup

SERVES 4 • 🥣 • TIME: 50 MINUTES

This soup feels extra special to me. Not only does it use butternut squash, my favorite fall vegetable, but it also contains one of my favorite flavor combos — Cheddar and apple. Since vegan products are more mainstream now, you can find shredded vegan Cheddar cheese at most well-stocked major grocery stores.

2 tbsp (30 mL) vegetable oil
½ onion, chopped
1 apple, peeled and chopped
3 cups (750 mL) cubed butternut squash
1 tsp (5 mL) dried sage
¼ tsp (1 mL) dried thyme

Salt and black pepper
2 cups (500 mL) low-sodium vegetable broth
1 cup (250 mL) shredded vegan Cheddar cheese

Blender or immersion blender

1. Heat the vegetable oil in a large pot over medium heat. Add the onion; cook for about 5 minutes, stirring frequently, until translucent. Add the apple, squash, sage, thyme and a sprinkle of salt and pepper; stir to combine. Add the broth; increase the heat to high and bring to a boil. Reduce the heat to medium-low and simmer for 30 minutes, stirring occasionally, until the squash is fork-tender.

2. Working in batches, transfer the soup to a blender. Remove the plug in the lid and lightly cover the hole with a clean dish towel. Blend on medium-low speed for 1 minute, until smooth. (You can also use an immersion blender in the pot.)

3. Transfer the soup back to the pot, over medium-low heat. Add the vegan Cheddar cheese; stir constantly for about 1 minute, until melted. Serve immediately or store in an airtight container in the fridge for up to 4 days.

chipotle corn chowder

SERVES 4 • ⬤ • TIME: 35 MINUTES

I know it's not traditional to add ground chipotle pepper to chowder, but sometimes when you venture outside of tradition, the result is pretty darn good! This chowder is every bit as rich as your grandma's dairy-heavy chowder, but it's made vegan by using coconut milk. The chipotle adds a slight bit of spice and gorgeous color.

2 tbsp (30 mL) vegetable oil
½ onion, diced
2 garlic cloves, minced
1 large white potato, peeled and cubed
4 cups (1 L) frozen corn kernels
1 tsp (5 mL) dried thyme
½ tsp (2 mL) salt

½ tsp (2 mL) black pepper
½ tsp (2 mL) ground chipotle pepper
1 can (14 oz/398 mL) full-fat coconut milk
1½ cups (375 mL) low-sodium vegetable broth
¼ cup (60 mL) chopped green onions

Blender or immersion blender

1. Heat the vegetable oil in a large pot over medium heat. Add the onion and garlic; cook for about 5 minutes, until the onion is translucent.

2. Add the potato; cook for 3 minutes, stirring frequently, until softened slightly. Add the corn; cook for 2 minutes, stirring frequently, until thawed.

3. Add the thyme, salt, pepper, chipotle pepper, coconut milk and broth; stir to combine. Increase the heat to high and bring to a boil. Reduce the heat to medium-low and simmer for about 15 minutes, stirring occasionally, until the potatoes are fork-tender.

4. Transfer half the chowder to a blender. Remove the plug in the lid and lightly cover the hole with a clean dish towel. Pulse until mostly smooth. (You can also use an immersion blender in the pot, but make sure to leave some chunks in the soup.)

5. Transfer the soup back into the pot; stir to combine. Heat over medium-low for 5 minutes, stirring frequently, until warm. Serve immediately or store in an airtight container in the fridge for up to 4 days. When ready to serve, divide among bowls and top with green onion.

split pea soup

SERVES 4 • ⬤ • TIME: 1 HOUR 20 MINUTES

I first came up with this recipe for a series on my YouTube channel called "The Deli Series" — a collection of videos showcasing deli-style sandwich-and-side combos. Traditional split pea soup often contains ham, but I'm convinced it's just as good made vegan-style. These tender simmered split peas and comforting spices are so flavorful, you won't miss the meat!

2 tbsp (30 mL) vegetable oil
1 small onion, diced
1 cup (250 mL) diced celery
1 cup (250 mL) diced carrot
2 garlic cloves, minced
1 bay leaf

1 tsp (5 mL) dried thyme
Salt and black pepper
2 cups (500 mL) split green peas
4 cups (1 L) low-sodium vegetable broth (approx.)

1. Heat the vegetable oil in large pot over medium heat. Add the onion, celery and carrot; cook, stirring frequently, for about 5 minutes or until the onion is translucent and the carrot and celery have softened slightly.

2. Add the garlic, bay leaf, thyme, ½ tsp (2 mL) salt and a sprinkle of pepper; cook for 2 minutes, stirring constantly, until fragrant.

3. Add the split peas and broth; stir to combine. Increase the heat to high and bring to a boil. Reduce the heat to medium-low; cover and simmer for about 1 hour, stirring occasionally, until the peas have softened and are starting to break apart. Add more broth while cooking if the peas start to stick to the bottom of the pot or the soup gets too thick.

4. Taste and add a sprinkle of salt and pepper, if desired. Discard the bay leaf. Serve immediately or store in an airtight container in the fridge for up to 4 days.

silky sweet potato soup

SERVES 4 • 🌑 • TIME: 30 MINUTES

Who can resist a creamy sweet potato soup? I know I can't. Sweet potatoes by nature are, well, *sweet*, but in this soup their sweetness is enhanced by my favorite Canadian staple, maple syrup. It's so velvety, and begs to be sopped up with a thick slice of sourdough bread!

1 tbsp (15 mL) vegetable oil

3 large sweet potatoes, peeled and chopped

1 tsp (5 mL) dried thyme

1 tsp (5 mL) dried sage

¼ tsp (1 mL) garlic powder

¼ tsp (1 mL) onion powder

Salt and black pepper

2 cups (500 mL) low-sodium vegetable broth

1 cup (250 mL) full-fat coconut milk

3 tbsp (45 mL) pure maple syrup

1 tsp (5 mL) ground cinnamon

Blender or immersion blender

1. Heat the vegetable oil in a large pot over medium heat. Add the sweet potatoes, thyme, sage, garlic powder, onion powder and a sprinkle of salt and pepper; cook for 3 minutes, stirring frequently, until softened slightly.

2. Add the broth and coconut milk; increase the heat to high and bring to a boil. Reduce the heat to medium-low; simmer for about 15 minutes, stirring occasionally, until the potato is soft and the soup has thickened.

3. Working in batches, transfer the soup to a blender, reserving the pot. Remove the plug in the lid and lightly cover the hole with a clean dish towel. Blend on low speed for 1 minute, until smooth. (You can also use an immersion blender in the pot.)

4. Transfer the soup back into the pot, over medium-low heat. Add the maple syrup and cinnamon; stir to combine. Heat for 5 minutes, stirring frequently, until warm. Serve immediately or store in an airtight container in the fridge for up to 4 days.

rustic tomato & white bean soup

SERVES 4 • **5** ● • TIME: 45 MINUTES

Growing up, the only tomato soup I ever had came from a can. My family made other soups from scratch but for some reason never made homemade tomato soup. My version is a bit thicker than a typical canned tomato soup because I like to add beans, which make it more substantial. I love serving it with a grilled cheese sandwich for dipping. If you want to get really fancy and creative, cut the grilled cheese into bite-size pieces and plop a few on top — grilled cheese croutons!

¼ cup (60 mL) vegan butter

1 onion, roughly chopped

2 cans (each 28 oz/796 mL) diced tomatoes (with juice)

1 can (14 oz/398 mL) white beans, such as cannellini, drained and rinsed

2 cups (500 mL) water

2 tsp (10 mL) dried basil

Pinch salt

Blender or immersion blender

1. Melt the vegan butter in a large pot over medium heat. Add the onion and cook for about 5 minutes, stirring occasionally, until translucent.

2. Add the tomatoes (with juice), white beans and water; stir to combine. Increase the heat to high and bring to a boil. Reduce the heat to medium-low; cover and simmer for 30 minutes, stirring occasionally, until slightly thickened.

3. Working in batches, transfer the soup to a blender, reserving the pot. Remove the plug in the lid and lightly cover the hole with a clean dish towel. Blend on low speed for 1 minute, until smooth. (You can also use an immersion blender in the pot.)

4. Transfer the soup back into the pot, over medium-low heat. Add the basil and salt; stir to combine. Heat, stirring frequently, for about 2 minutes, until warm. Serve immediately or store in an airtight container in the fridge for up to 4 days.

summery zucchini carpaccio

SERVES 4 TO 6 • 🥗 • TIME: 15 MINUTES

I had never thought to eat zucchini raw until very recently, when I ordered a zucchini salad at a restaurant in Halifax. And while this recipe may sound fancy, I promise you it isn't! The trick is to peel the zucchini with a mandoline or vegetable peeler, which makes the salad look beautiful and keeps each bite super light. It's now my new favorite for summer picnics and potlucks, and a nice change from the typical leafy green salad.

¼ cup (60 mL) extra-virgin olive oil
2 tsp (10 mL) Dijon mustard
2 tsp (10 mL) pure maple syrup
¼ tsp (1 mL) garlic powder
Pinch salt

3 zucchini, sliced into ribbons (see my tip)
¼ cup (60 mL) chopped walnuts or whole pine nuts
2 tbsp (30 mL) finely chopped fresh basil

1. Whisk together the olive oil, Dijon mustard, maple syrup, garlic powder and salt in a large serving bowl.

2. Add the zucchini and walnuts; toss to coat. Let stand for 5 minutes or store in the fridge for up to 12 hours. Top with basil just before serving.

my tip Making zucchini ribbons is much easier than it looks! If you have a mandoline, use it here, but a vegetable peeler is also super simple. Hold the peeler against one side of the zucchini and gently peel it into strips. Peel 2 to 3 times on one side, then rotate the zucchini a quarter-turn and repeat. Keep turning and peeling until most of the zucchini has been turned into ribbons and only a tiny section remains.

the classic potato salad

SERVES 4 • **5** • TIME: 30 MINUTES
(PLUS 1 HOUR FOR CHILLING)

I have made this potato salad recipe so many times I've honestly lost count. It's always a great choice in the summertime when I want a side to go with BBQ veggie burgers. The ingredients list looks basic, but the salad packs a ton of delicious tangy flavor. If you want to jazz it up, see my tip for some ideas.

5 medium red potatoes, chopped
½ cup (125 mL) vegan mayonnaise
1 tsp (5 mL) white vinegar

1 tsp (5 mL) Dijon mustard
1 tbsp (15 mL) organic cane sugar
Pinch salt

1. Place the potatoes in a large pot and cover with about 2 inches (5 cm) water. Bring to a boil over high heat and cook for about 10 minutes, until fork-tender. Drain and rinse under cold water until cool. Let stand in the colander until dry.

2. Meanwhile, whisk together the vegan mayonnaise, vinegar, Dijon mustard, sugar and salt in a large serving bowl. Add the potatoes; stir gently to coat.

3. Cover and transfer to the fridge to chill for at least 1 hour or up to 4 days. Serve.

my tip If you want to jazz up this recipe, try adding ½ tsp (2 mL) chili powder with the vegan mayonnaise and ¼ cup (60 mL) chopped celery and/or sliced green onion with the potatoes. The chili powder will give it some kick, and celery and green onion add some crunch.

roasted kale & brussels caesar-esque salad

SERVES 4 • ⬢ • TIME: 45 MINUTES

If you're like me and don't love a raw kale salad, definitely give this recipe a try. It's a play on the traditional Caesar. The kale, which is normally a fairly tough leafy green, is roasted for a few minutes to soften it, making it much more palatable. The tofu crumbles are seasoned to taste like bacon bits and it's topped with a super-creamy, nut-free dressing. Dreamy, if you ask me!

Baked Tofu Crumbles
1 cup (250 mL) firm tofu, crumbled
2 tbsp (30 mL) low-sodium soy sauce
1 tbsp (15 mL) pure maple syrup
½ tsp (2 mL) liquid smoke or smoked paprika

Brussels & Kale
2 cups (500 mL) thinly sliced Brussels sprouts (about 8 oz/250 g)

6 cups (1.5 L) finely chopped kale, ribs removed (about 1 bunch)
3 tbsp (45 mL) vegetable oil
Pinch of salt
1 recipe Sunflower Caesar Dressing (page 28)

Large rimmed baking sheet

1. Preheat the oven to 425°F (220°C).

2. **BAKED TOFU CRUMBLES** Combine the tofu, soy sauce, maple syrup and liquid smoke in a small bowl; stir to coat. Spread on the baking sheet in an even layer. Bake in the preheated oven for about 10 minutes, until the tofu starts to brown.

3. **BRUSSELS & KALE** Push the tofu to one side and spread the Brussels sprouts and kale on the baking sheet. (The kale doesn't need to be in a single layer because it will shrivel while it cooks.) Drizzle the oil overtop the vegetables and sprinkle with salt; stir gently to coat. Bake for about 10 minutes, stirring halfway through, until the tofu is golden and the Brussels sprouts are fork-tender.

4. Remove the baking sheet from the oven. Transfer the roasted vegetables to a large serving bowl. Pour the dressing overtop; toss gently to coat. Sprinkle the tofu crumbles overtop. Serve immediately.

chopped cucumber salad

SERVES 4 • 5 • TIME: 10 MINUTES

I love a zesty fresh side salad, especially in the summer! This is the perfect dish for a barbecue or potluck, because it's quick to make ahead of time and it's really easy to double or triple the recipe to serve a larger crowd.

¼ cup (60 mL) seasoned rice wine vinegar
2 tsp (10 mL) sesame oil
1 tsp (5 mL) pure maple syrup

Pinch salt
2 large cucumbers, diced
½ red onion, finely chopped

1. Add the rice wine vinegar, sesame oil, maple syrup and salt to a large serving bowl; whisk to combine.

2. Add the cucumber and red onion; toss to combine.

3. Chill in the fridge for at least 1 hour or up to 4 days. Serve.

my tip If you want to elevate this simple but beyond-tasty salad, try adding ½ tsp (2 mL) hot pepper flakes and 1 tsp (5 mL) sesame seeds in Step 2.

warm chickpea & quinoa salad

SERVES 4 • 5 ⬤ • TIME: 25 MINUTES

When I first went vegan and had no idea what to eat, my go-to quick lunch became quinoa with steamed spinach, lemon juice, salt and pepper. It was easy and satisfying and made me feel really good. This is a slightly heartier version of that simple meal since I've swapped out the spinach for chickpeas and green peas. It's filling enough to be enjoyed on its own, if that's your thing.

1½ cups (375 mL) quinoa

1 cup (250 mL) frozen green peas, thawed

1 cup (250 mL) cooked chickpeas, drained and rinsed

2 tbsp (30 mL) extra-virgin olive oil

2 tbsp (30 mL) freshly squeezed lemon juice

Pinch salt

1. Cook the quinoa according to the package directions. Fluff, then turn heat to medium-low.

2. Add the green peas, chickpeas, olive oil, lemon juice and salt; stir to combine. Heat for about 2 minutes, stirring frequently, until warm. Serve immediately or store in an airtight container in the fridge for up to 5 days.

my tip This salad is very simple, but when I want to take it up a notch, I make a batch of Spiced Tahini Sauce (page 22) and substitute it for the olive oil, lemon juice and salt. It adds such a nice richness and hint of spice!

mains

bbq king oyster "pulled pork" sandwiches

SERVES 4 • 5 • TIME: 25 MINUTES

Growing up, one of my favorite summer meals was pulled pork sandwiches. Now I opt for this amazing mushroom version. By shredding the king oyster mushrooms and cooking them with spices and BBQ sauce, you can create a vegan "pulled pork" that is perfect for sandwiches! These taste great on their own, but I also love to add toppings such as shredded lettuce, vegan mayo and hot sauce.

6 large king oyster mushrooms
½ onion, thinly sliced
2 tbsp (30 mL) vegetable oil, divided
¾ cup (175 mL) store-bought vegan BBQ sauce

Salt and black pepper
4 hamburger buns

Large rimmed baking sheet, lined with parchment paper

1. Preheat the oven to 400°F (200°C).

2. Using two forks or your fingers, shred the mushrooms into thin pieces.

3. Spread the mushrooms and onion on the prepared baking sheet in an even layer. Drizzle 1 tbsp (15 mL) vegetable oil overtop and stir gently to coat. Bake in the preheated oven for about 8 minutes, until mushrooms are slightly shrunken and starting to brown. Remove the baking sheet from the oven.

4. Heat the remaining 1 tbsp (15 mL) vegetable oil in a large frying pan over medium heat. Add the roasted mushrooms and onion and cook for about 5 minutes, stirring frequently, until browned. Add the vegan BBQ sauce, salt and pepper; stir to coat. Cook for 3 minutes, stirring constantly, until the sauce starts to thicken.

5. Divide the mushroom mixture among the buns. Serve.

my tip You can find king oyster mushrooms at most well-stocked grocery stores and Asian supermarkets.

one-pot mushroom stroganoff

SERVES 4 • ⬤ • TIME: 40 MINUTES

Lazy cooks, rejoice! Although stroganoff is like a stew served over pasta, my version is made in one pot, saving you from washing a lot of dishes. This recipe uses mushrooms instead of beef, and the coconut milk and lemon juice replace the sour cream you will find in traditional stroganoffs. It's an ultra-comforting winter dinner.

1 tbsp (15 mL) vegan butter
½ onion, finely chopped
2 garlic cloves, minced
½ cup (125 mL) dry white wine (see my tip)
2 cups (500 mL) sliced cremini mushrooms
4 cups (1 L) rotini pasta
3 cups (750 mL) low-sodium vegetable broth

1 cup (250 mL) full-fat coconut milk
3 tbsp (45 mL) tahini
2 tbsp (30 mL) freshly squeezed lemon juice
½ tsp (2 mL) dried thyme
Salt and black pepper
Lemon wedges

1. Melt the vegan butter in a large pot over medium heat. Add the onion and garlic; cook for about 5 minutes, stirring frequently, until the onion is translucent. Add the white wine and cook for about 3 minutes, stirring frequently, until mostly evaporated.

2. Add the mushrooms and cook for about 4 minutes, stirring frequently, until softened.

3. Add the rotini, vegetable stock, coconut milk, tahini, lemon juice, thyme and a sprinkle of salt and pepper; stir to combine. Increase the heat to high and bring to a boil. Reduce the heat to medium-low, cover and simmer for 10 minutes or until the pasta is cooked.

4. Season with salt and pepper to taste. Serve with lemon wedges alongside.

my tip If you're wondering what dry white wine to use, stick to a Sauvignon Blanc or Pinot Grigio for best results.

creamy tofu tomato curry

SERVES 4 • ⬤ • TIME: 35 MINUTES

Are you craving Indian food? This recipe was inspired by the Indian dish butter chicken, which is a chicken curry cooked in a tomato cream sauce. I replace the chicken with firm tofu and use blended cooked cashews to mimic the richness of butter and cream. I love serving it over fluffy basmati rice.

1 tbsp (15 mL) vegetable oil
1 medium onion, diced
1 tsp (5 mL) ground turmeric
1 tsp (5 mL) ground cumin
1 tsp (5 mL) garam masala
1 tsp (5 mL) ground coriander
1 tsp (5 mL) salt
1 tsp (5 mL) organic cane sugar
3 garlic cloves, minced

1 can (14 oz/398 mL) diced tomatoes (with juice)
½ cup (125 mL) raw cashews
½ cup (125 mL) water
12 oz (375 g) firm tofu, cubed
2 tbsp (30 mL) chopped fresh cilantro (optional)

High-powered blender
or food processor

1. Heat the vegetable oil in a large pot over medium heat. Add the onion; cook for about 5 minutes, stirring frequently, until translucent.

2. Add the turmeric, cumin, garam masala, coriander, salt, sugar and garlic; stir to combine. Cook for 1 minute, stirring constantly, until fragrant.

3. Add the tomatoes (with juice), cashews and water. Simmer for about 8 minutes, stirring occasionally, until the mixture has thickened slightly.

4. Remove from the heat and let cool slightly. Transfer to a high-powered blender, reserving the pot. Remove the plug in the blender lid and cover the hole lightly with a clean dish towel to allow the steam to escape. Blend on low speed for about 2 minutes, until smooth.

5. Spoon the curry sauce back into the pot and add the tofu; stir to combine. Bring to a simmer over medium heat for 5 minutes, stirring frequently, until heated through. Top with cilantro (if using); serve.

my tip If you have some extra time or don't mind dirtying another dish, you can make the tofu crispy. Place it on a large baking sheet lined with parchment paper and bake in an oven preheated to 400°F (200°C) for 15 minutes, flipping halfway through, until golden.

peach & lentil curry

SERVES 4 • ⬤ • TIME: 25 MINUTES

I first tried dal at a great Indian restaurant in Halifax called Dhaba Express and immediately fell in love. This recipe, though not traditional, was inspired by one of their amazing dals. I simmer split red lentils with spices, broth and coconut milk and use peaches for a pop of added sweetness. Feel free to replace the peaches (when not in season) with an equal amount of chopped dried apricots, which are much easier to find during the colder months. I like to serve this dish over basmati rice.

2 tbsp (30 mL) olive oil, divided

1 onion, finely chopped

2 garlic cloves, minced

2 tsp (10 mL) curry powder

½ tsp (2 mL) fennel seeds

½ tsp (2 mL) cumin seeds

½ tsp (2 mL) ground coriander

2 ripe peaches, peeled and chopped (about ¾ cup/175 mL)

½ cup (125 mL) dried split red lentils

1 can (14 oz/398 mL) full-fat coconut milk

1 cup (250 mL) low-sodium vegetable broth

1 tsp (5 mL) salt (approx.)

2 tbsp (30 mL) freshly squeezed lemon juice

1. Heat 1 tbsp (15 mL) olive oil in a large pot over medium heat. Add the onion and garlic; cook for about 5 minutes, stirring frequently, until the onion is translucent.

2. Add the remaining 1 tbsp (15 mL) olive oil, curry powder, fennel seeds, cumin seeds and coriander; stir to combine. Cook for about 1 minute, stirring constantly, until fragrant. Add the peaches, lentils, coconut milk and broth; stir to combine. Cover and reduce the heat to medium-low. Gently simmer for about 10 minutes, stirring frequently, until the lentils are cooked and the curry sauce has thickened.

3. Add the salt and lemon juice; stir to combine. Taste and adjust the salt, if desired. Let cool slightly before serving.

my tip You can store this curry in an airtight container in the fridge for up to 5 days or in the freezer for up to 3 months. To reheat, thaw overnight in the fridge, if frozen. Add to a large pot and cook over medium heat for about 10 minutes, stirring frequently, until warmed through.

herb risotto with parmesan sprinkle

SERVES 4 • 🍲 • TIME: 45 MINUTES

Risotto sounds so fancy — I always feel like I'm at a nice restaurant when I make it at home! It tends to be more hands-on than the average one-pot recipe because of all the stirring, but it's so worth it. This version is packed full of fragrant fresh herbs that add a burst of flavor in every bite. I like to serve this with some garlic bread on the side.

2 tbsp (30 mL) olive oil

½ onion, finely chopped

1¼ cups (310 mL) Arborio rice

4 cups (1 L) low-sodium vegetable broth

¼ cup (60 mL) lightly packed finely chopped fresh basil

¼ cup (60 mL) lightly packed finely chopped fresh dill

¼ cup (60 mL) lightly packed finely chopped parsley

¼ cup (60 mL) lightly packed finely chopped fresh chives

2 tbsp (30 mL) freshly squeezed lemon juice

Salt and black pepper

4 tsp (20 mL) Herb & Garlic Parmesan Sprinkle (page 27) or store-bought vegan Parmesan cheese (see my tip)

1. Heat the olive oil in a large pot over medium heat. Add the onion; cook for about 5 minutes, stirring frequently, until translucent.

2. Add the rice and cook for about 3 minutes, stirring constantly, until golden. Add ½ cup (125 mL) broth and cook for about 5 minutes, stirring constantly, until the broth is absorbed. Continue adding the broth ½ cup (125 mL) at a time, stirring constantly and adjusting the heat to maintain a simmer, until the rice is al dente, about 30 minutes.

3. Add the basil, dill, parsley, chives, lemon juice and a sprinkle of salt and pepper; cook for 1 minute, stirring constantly, until the herbs are slightly wilted.

4. Remove from the heat and divide among 4 bowls. Top with Herb & Garlic Parmesan Sprinkle and some extra pepper.

my tip If you're using store-bought vegan Parmesan, add ¼ tsp (1 mL) garlic powder in Step 2, right before adding the broth.

simple squash risotto

SERVES 4 • **5** • TIME: 1 HOUR

This risotto is loosely adapted from a recipe my mom used to make. Now whenever I make it, the classic combination of sage and squash takes me right back to Sunday dinners at my parents' house. If you're feeling extra fancy you can use fried fresh sage as a garnish (see my tips).

4 cups (1 L) peeled and cubed butternut squash
Vegetable oil for cooking
Salt and black pepper
½ onion, finely chopped
1¼ cups (310 mL) Arborio rice (see my tips)

4 cups (1 L) low-sodium vegetable broth
1 tsp (5 mL) dried sage

Large rimmed baking sheet, lined with parchment paper

1. Preheat the oven to 400°F (200°C).

2. Place the squash on the prepared baking sheet. Drizzle with 2 tbsp (30 mL) vegetable oil and sprinkle with salt and pepper. Bake in the preheated oven for 35 minutes, flipping halfway through, until the squash is fork-tender. Set aside.

3. Meanwhile, add 1 tbsp (15 mL) vegetable oil and the onion to a large pot over medium heat; cook for about 5 minutes, stirring frequently, until the onion is translucent. Add the rice and cook for 3 minutes, stirring constantly, until golden.

4. Add ½ cup (125 mL) broth and cook for about 5 minutes, until the broth is absorbed. Continue adding broth ½ cup (125 mL) at a time, stirring constantly and adjusting the heat to keep it at a simmer, until the rice is al dente, about 30 minutes.

5. Add the cooked squash, sage and a sprinkle of salt and pepper; stir to combine. Serve.

my tips Arborio rice is necessary for making risotto — there are no substitutes. You can find it at most well-stocked grocery stores and bulk food stores.

If I have extra time, I put 2 tbsp (30 mL) chopped fresh sage in a small frying pan with 1 tsp (5 mL) vegan butter and lightly fry it over medium heat for about 3 minutes, until crispy. Add it just before serving — it makes a great garnish for this risotto!

liv's famous one-pot mac & cheese

SERVES 4 • ⬡ • TIME: 25 MINUTES

This recipe became an instant hit on my YouTube channel and blog. I think part of the appeal is that it's a one-pot wonder, but once people try it, they are completely hooked! Think of this more as a three-cheese mac and cheese: the tahini, nutritional yeast and vegan Cheddar all add slightly different flavors, making this dish so much more complex than the traditional stuff. As a bonus, it's nut free, unlike most vegan mac and cheeses.

4 cups (1 L) dry macaroni

2 tsp (10 mL) Dijon mustard

1 tsp (5 mL) salt

½ tsp (2 mL) garlic powder

6 cups (1.5 L) water

1 cup (250 mL) unsweetened nondairy milk

⅔ cup (150 mL) nutritional yeast

¼ cup (60 mL) freshly squeezed lemon juice

2 tbsp (30 mL) tahini

2 cups (500 mL) shredded vegan Cheddar cheese

Black pepper

1. Add the macaroni, Dijon mustard, salt, garlic powder and water to a large pot over medium-high heat, stirring to combine. Bring to a boil, then cook for about 8 minutes, until almost all the water is dissolved and the pasta is al dente. Do not drain.

2. Add the nondairy milk, nutritional yeast, lemon juice and tahini; stir until combined. Add the vegan Cheddar cheese; stir constantly for about 2 minutes, until melted.

3. Let cool slightly before dividing among the bowls. Top each with pepper; serve.

chili cheese macaroni

SERVES 4 • ⬤ • TIME: 35 MINUTES

Chili is a meal on its own, but can also play a supporting role to elevate other foods: think chili cheese fries, chili dogs or this amazing chili mac and cheese! This recipe is packed with fiber and protein but tastes like a super indulgent meal. It combines the warming, spicy flavors of chili with the rich creaminess of a homemade mac and cheese.

1 tbsp (15 mL) vegetable oil

1 onion, finely chopped

1 red bell pepper, chopped

2 garlic cloves, minced

1 can (14 oz/398 mL) red kidney beans, drained and rinsed

1 cup (250 mL) vegan ground beef

2 tbsp (30 mL) chili powder

2 tsp (10 mL) ground coriander

1 tsp (5 mL) salt (approx.)

½ tsp (2 mL) black pepper (approx.)

1 can (28 oz/796 mL) crushed tomatoes (with juice)

1½ cups (375 mL) low-sodium vegetable broth

2 cups (500 mL) macaroni

2 cups (500 mL) shredded vegan Cheddar cheese

1. Heat the vegetable oil in a large pot over medium heat. Add the onion, bell pepper and garlic; cook for about 5 minutes, stirring frequently, until the onion is translucent and the pepper has softened.

2. Add the kidney beans, vegan ground beef, chili powder, coriander, salt, pepper, crushed tomatoes (with juice), broth and macaroni; stir to combine. Increase the heat to medium-high and bring to a boil. Reduce the heat to medium-low, cover and simmer for 10 to 12 minutes or until the macaroni is al dente.

3. Stir in half of the vegan Cheddar cheese. Adjust the salt and pepper to taste. Top with the remaining Cheddar cheese; cover and cook for about 1 minute, until the cheese has melted. Divide among 4 bowls and serve.

> **my tip** Store leftovers in an airtight container in the fridge for up to 4 days or in the freezer for up to 3 months. To reheat, thaw overnight in the fridge, if frozen. Transfer to a microwave-safe bowl and microwave on Medium for 2 minutes, until heated through.

grown-up nuggets & fries

SERVES 4 • • TIME: 1 HOUR

In this more "grown-up" version of nuggets and fries, panko-breaded tofu replaces the chicken, the potatoes are baked instead of fried, and I've added an extra side of veg to round out the meal.

Tofu Nuggets

12 oz (375 g) firm tofu
½ cup (125 mL) unsweetened nondairy milk
½ cup (125 mL) panko bread crumbs
¼ cup (60 mL) all-purpose flour
2 tbsp (30 mL) nutritional yeast
½ tsp (2 mL) black pepper

Chipotle Potato Wedges

2 large russet potatoes, sliced into wedges

1 tbsp (15 mL) vegetable oil
1 tsp (5 mL) ground chipotle black pepper
Salt and black pepper

Garlic Cherry Tomatoes

1 cup (250 mL) cherry tomatoes, halved
1 garlic clove, minced
1 tbsp (15 mL) vegetable oil
Pinch salt

Large rimmed baking sheet, lined with parchment paper

1. Preheat the oven to 400°F (200°C).

2. **TOFU NUGGETS** Place the tofu on a clean folded dish towel. Place another clean, folded dish towel on top, followed by a large pot or frying pan. Let stand for 5 to 10 minutes.

3. Slice the tofu in half lengthwise, then slice each half into 6 pieces.

4. Meanwhile, pour the nondairy milk into a medium bowl. In a separate medium bowl, whisk together the panko crumbs, flour, nutritional yeast and pepper. Working in batches, dip the tofu pieces into the nondairy milk, then into the panko mixture, turning to coat all sides. Place on the prepared baking sheet. Discard excess nondairy milk and panko mixture.

5. **CHIPOTLE POTATO WEDGES** Place the potatoes, vegetable oil, chipotle pepper and a sprinkle of salt and pepper in a large bowl; toss to coat. Add to the baking sheet, reserving the bowl. Bake tofu and potatoes in the preheated oven for 20 minutes.

6. **GARLIC CHERRY TOMATOES** Meanwhile, place the cherry tomatoes, garlic, vegetable oil and a sprinkle of salt in the reserved bowl; toss to coat. Set aside.

7. Flip the potatoes and tofu. Add tomatoes to baking sheet and bake for another 15 to 20 minutes, until potatoes are fork-tender and tofu is golden. Remove from the oven; serve.

creamy carrot shells

SERVES 4 • **5** • TIME: 35 MINUTES

I love pasta because you can hide vegetables in it so easily. This sauce is packed with carrots, but apart from its vibrant color, you'd never know. It tastes like a garlicky cream sauce with a slight sweetness, so it's sure to be a hit with picky eaters and proclaimed veggie haters!

3 cups (750 mL) small-shell pasta
Water
1 tbsp (15 mL) vegetable oil
½ onion, diced
2 garlic cloves, chopped

3 large carrots, chopped
½ cup (125 mL) raw cashews
Pinch salt

High-powered blender
or food processor

1. Cook the pasta according to the package directions. Drain and set aside.

2. Meanwhile, add the vegetable oil, onion and garlic to a large pot over medium heat. Cook for about 5 minutes, stirring frequently, until the onion is translucent. Transfer to a small bowl, reserving the pot. Set aside.

3. Add the carrots, cashews and 1½ cups (375 mL) water to the pot over high heat; boil for 10 to 12 minutes, until the carrots are fork-tender. Let cool slightly.

4. Transfer the carrot mixture, including the water, to a high-powered blender (see my tips), reserving the pot. Add the onion mixture and salt; blend on low speed for about 2 minutes, until smooth.

5. Combine the cooked pasta and carrot sauce in the reserved pot. Return to medium-low heat. Cook for about 3 minutes, stirring frequently, until the sauce thickens slightly.

6. Remove from the heat and let cool slightly. Divide among 4 bowls; serve.

my tips This pasta is great as is, but if you prefer a cheesy flavor (or are serving it to kids!), try adding ¼ cup (60 mL) nutritional yeast to the blender in Step 4. It definitely amps up the flavor and adds a little extra something!

When you're blending a hot liquid, make sure to remove the plug in the blender lid and lightly cover the hole with a clean dish towel, leaving room for the steam to escape.

tempeh & roasted veggie bowl with pesto

SERVES 4 • ⬦ • TIME: 45 MINUTES

The combination of nutty soy-glazed tempeh and herby, garlicky pesto-covered veggies may seem an unlikely combination, but trust me, it works! This recipe can be served as written, but I often add some brown rice or quinoa alongside. The roast veggies and tempeh keep well in the fridge for a few days (see my tip), so it's a great option for meal prep.

2 cups (500 mL) cubed tempeh
2 tbsp (30 mL) reduced-sodium soy sauce
4 zucchini, chopped
4 carrots, chopped
2 red bell peppers, chopped
2 tbsp (30 mL) vegetable oil

1 red onion, sliced
Salt and black pepper
⅔ cup (150 mL) Basil & Walnut Pesto (page 24) or store-bought vegan pesto

Two large rimmed baking sheets, lined with parchment paper

1. Preheat the oven to 375°F (190°C).

2. Place the tempeh and soy sauce in a large bowl; toss to coat. Spread on the prepared baking sheet, reserving the bowl.

3. Add the zucchini, carrots, bell peppers, onion, vegetable oil and a sprinkle of salt and pepper to the reserved bowl; toss to coat. Divide evenly between the prepared baking sheets.

4. Bake in the preheated oven for 10 minutes, until the vegetables begin to soften and brown.

5. Remove from the oven, stir and bake for 10 to 15 minutes more, until the carrots are fork-tender and the tempeh is browned.

6. Remove from the oven, add the pesto and stir gently to coat. Serve.

my tip Store leftovers in an airtight container in the fridge for up to 4 days. To reheat, microwave on Medium for 2 minutes, until heated through.

pizza with white sauce, balsamic onions & spinach

SERVES 4 • ⬭ • TIME: 30 MINUTES

We have pizza at least once a week. Sometimes I get tired of regular tomato sauce, though, and that's when this recipe comes in handy. A creamy white sauce made from cashews is a lovely change, and it's the perfect base for balsamic onions and spinach.

White Sauce
1 cup (250 mL) raw cashews
1 garlic clove
¾ cup (175 mL) water
1 tsp (5 mL) white vinegar or apple cider vinegar
½ tsp (2 mL) salt

Pizza
1 tbsp (15 mL) vegetable oil
½ red onion, thinly sliced
1 garlic clove, minced
¼ tsp (1 mL) organic cane sugar

2 tsp (10 mL) balsamic vinegar
2 cups (500 mL) lightly packed chopped baby spinach
1 ball (1 lb/500 g) store-bought pizza dough or 1 recipe Pizza Dough (page 84), prepared through Step 3
2 cups (500 mL) vegan mozzarella cheese shreds
Black pepper

High-powered blender

13- by 9-inch (33 by 23 cm) rimmed baking sheet (see my tip), lined with parchment paper

1. Preheat the oven to 425°F (220°C).

2. **WHITE SAUCE** Combine the cashews, garlic, water, vinegar and salt in a high-powered blender. Blend on high speed for about 2 minutes, until completely smooth. Set aside.

3. **PIZZA** Heat the vegetable oil in a large frying pan over medium heat. Add the onion; cook for about 5 minutes, until translucent. Add the garlic, sugar and balsamic vinegar; cook for about 2 minutes, until the onion is browned. Add the spinach and cook for 1 minute, until wilted. Set aside.

4. Press the dough onto the prepared baking sheet in an even layer. Spread the white sauce overtop in an even layer, leaving a 1-inch (2.5 cm) border. Add the vegan mozzarella, followed by the onion-and-spinach mixture. Sprinkle with pepper.

5. Bake in the preheated oven for 15 minutes, until the bottom of the pizza is golden brown and the cheese is melted and bubbling. Remove from the oven and let cool slightly before slicing and serving.

my tip If you want your pizza to be round, use a round baking sheet or pizza stone.

sheet-pan lasagna

SERVES 4 • ⬦ • TIME: 45 MINUTES

If you thought lasagna was too labor-intensive for a weeknight dinner, this recipe will definitely surprise you. Although this lasagna may be thinner than you're used to, I love that you get crunchy edges and browned bits with every bite! Oven-ready noodles make this extra quick, so make sure you use them to save on cooking time.

1 tbsp (15 mL) vegetable oil
½ onion, finely chopped
1 cup (250 mL) vegan ground beef
1 cup (250 mL) chopped mushrooms
1 cup (250 mL) lightly packed
baby spinach

4 cups (1 L) store-bought marinara sauce
12 oven-ready lasagna noodles
2 cups (500 mL) vegan mozzarella
cheese shreds

13- by 9-inch (33 by 23 cm)
rimmed baking sheet, greased

1. Preheat the oven to 375°F (190°C).

2. Heat the vegetable oil in a large frying pan over medium heat. Add the onion, vegan ground beef and mushrooms; cook for 5 minutes, stirring frequently, until the onion is translucent. Add the spinach and cook for 1 minute, stirring constantly, until wilted.

3. Spread 1½ cups (375 mL) marinara sauce on the prepared baking sheet in an even layer. Add 6 noodles in an even layer. Top with 1½ cups (375 mL) marinara sauce, followed by the vegan ground beef mixture. Add the remaining 6 noodles on top in an even layer. Top with the remaining sauce, followed by the vegan mozzarella cheese.

4. Cover the baking sheet with foil. Bake in the preheated oven for 20 minutes.

5. Remove the foil, then bake for another 10 minutes, until the cheese is melted and the edges are brown and crispy.

6. Remove from the oven and let cool slightly before slicing and serving.

my tip Store presliced leftovers in an airtight container in the fridge for up to 4 days or in the freezer for up to 3 months. To reheat, thaw overnight in the fridge, if frozen. Place a slice of lasagna on a microwave-safe plate. Microwave on High for 2 minutes, until heated through.

"honey" garlic tofu & broccoli

SERVES 4 • ◇ • TIME: 25 MINUTES

If you are a fitness fanatic, you may be looking for high-protein vegan recipes. Both tofu and broccoli are great post-workout foods, and this recipe combines them with a scrumptious honey garlic–inspired sauce. This is a great meal on its own, but if I have some extra time, I cook some rice or quinoa to serve alongside.

12 oz (375 g) firm tofu, cubed

2 cups (500 mL) broccoli florets (see my tip)

½ onion, finely sliced

2 tbsp (30 mL) vegetable oil

Salt and black pepper

1 recipe "Honey" Garlic Sauce (page 23)

Large rimmed baking sheet, lined with parchment paper

1. Preheat the oven to 400°F (200°C).

2. Spread the tofu, broccoli and onion on the prepared baking sheet. Drizzle the vegetable oil overtop and sprinkle with salt and pepper. Stir gently to coat. Bake in the preheated oven for about 10 minutes or until the tofu starts to brown.

3. Remove the baking sheet from the oven and stir gently. Drizzle the "Honey" Garlic Sauce evenly overtop, then bake for about 8 minutes, until the sauce has thickened and the broccoli is fork-tender.

4. Remove from the oven and let cool slightly before serving.

my tip If you wish to use frozen broccoli, simply substitute 2 cups (500 mL) frozen broccoli florets for the fresh and proceed with the recipe as directed.

smoky broccoli, sweet potato & sausage tray bake

SERVES 4 • ◈ • TIME: 45 MINUTES

This recipe is great for weeknights because it requires minimal preparation and is done in less than 45 minutes — and most of that is hands-off cooking time. I make this dinner often because it's filling and healthy and, most important, tastes delicious!

2 large sweet potatoes (about 1 lb/500 g), peeled and cubed

½ red onion, sliced

2 tbsp (30 mL) vegetable oil, divided

2 tsp (10 mL) smoked paprika, divided

Salt and black pepper

1 broccoli head, chopped into florets

3 vegan sausages, sliced into rounds

Large rimmed baking sheet, lined with parchment paper

1. Preheat the oven to 400°F (200°C).

2. Place the sweet potatoes and onion in a large bowl. Add 1 tbsp (15 mL) vegetable oil, 1 tsp (5 mL) smoked paprika and a sprinkle of salt and pepper; toss to coat. Spread on the prepared baking sheet, reserving the bowl.

3. Bake in the preheated oven for 15 minutes.

4. Meanwhile, add the broccoli and sausage to the reserved bowl. Add the remaining 1 tbsp (15 mL) vegetable oil and 1 tsp (5 mL) smoked paprika, plus a sprinkle of salt and pepper. Set aside.

5. Remove the baking sheet from the oven; stir. Add the broccoli and vegan sausage to the baking sheet. Return to the oven and bake for another 15 minutes, until the sausage is browned and the broccoli and sweet potato are fork-tender.

6. Remove from the oven and sprinkle with pepper; serve.

eggplant parm

SERVES 4 • ⬭ • TIME: 1 HOUR

The eggplant here is crispy on the outside, tender on the inside, and can be eaten so many different ways. This recipe is delicious on its own, but you can also serve the eggplant on top of linguine or place a few slices in a burger bun to make a tasty sandwich.

½ cup (125 mL) unsweetened nondairy milk

1¼ cups (310 mL) panko bread crumbs

⅓ cup (75 mL) all-purpose flour

¼ cup (60 mL) vegan Parmesan cheese or nutritional yeast

¼ tsp (1 mL) salt

1 large eggplant (approx. 1 lb/500 g), sliced into 12 rounds ½ inch (1 cm) each

Cooking spray (optional)

1½ cups (375 mL) store-bought marinara sauce

2 cups (500 mL) vegan mozzarella cheese shreds

Large rimmed baking sheet, lined with parchment paper

1. Preheat the oven to 400°F (200°C).

2. Pour the nondairy milk into a large bowl. Set aside.

3. Whisk the panko, flour, vegan Parmesan and salt in a separate large bowl.

4. Submerge a slice of eggplant in the nondairy milk, then dip into the panko mixture, turning until all sides are coated. Gently shake off the excess crumbs. Place on the prepared baking sheet. Repeat with the remaining slices, making a single layer. Discard excess nondairy milk and panko mixture.

5. Spray the eggplant slices with cooking spray (if using). Bake in the preheated oven for 15 minutes or until golden brown on the bottom, then remove from the oven, flip and bake for 10 minutes more, until golden brown on the other side.

6. Spoon the marinara sauce evenly over the slices, then sprinkle with the vegan mozzarella cheese. Bake for 10 minutes or until cheese is melted. Remove from the oven and let cool slightly before serving.

my tip If you prefer the eggplant coating to stay crispy, skip adding the marinara sauce in Step 6. Sprinkle the vegan cheese directly over the eggplant and bake as directed. Meanwhile, heat the marinara sauce separately in a small pot over medium-low heat for about 5 minutes, stirring frequently, until warm. Spoon over the eggplant slices just before serving.

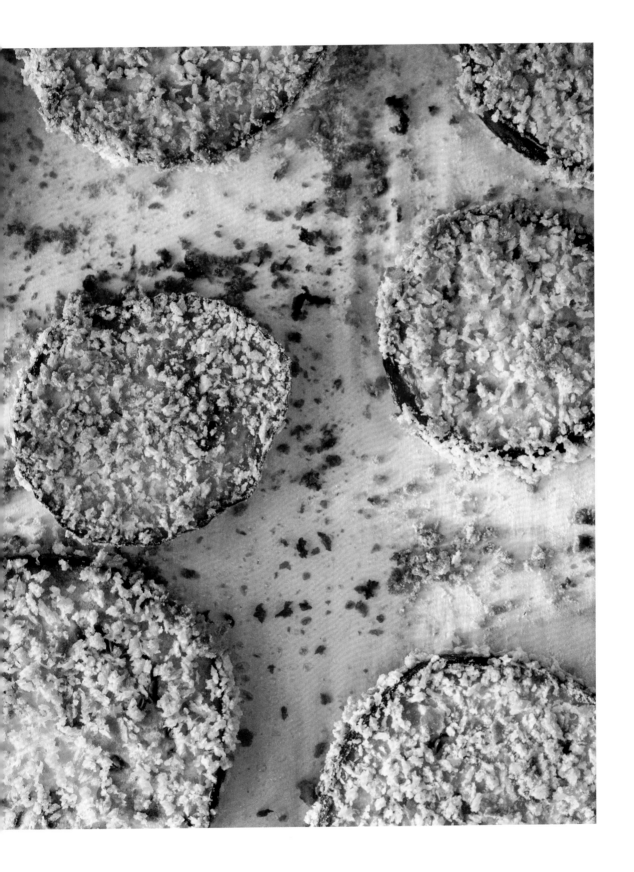

vodka penne

SERVES 4 • 🍷 • TIME: 50 MINUTES

If you read this title and wondered if it was a typo, it's not — this sauce really has vodka in it! I know, I was skeptical too. Why add vodka? For the same reason people cook with wine. It intensifies the flavors and amps up the whole dish. To keep this recipe vegan, I've switched out the usual butter and cream for vegan butter and coconut milk.

1 lb (500 g) penne pasta
¼ cup (60 mL) vegan butter
½ onion, diced
2 garlic cloves, minced
¼ cup (60 mL) vodka
1 jar (26 oz/700 mL) store-bought marinara sauce (see my tip)

1 can (14 oz /398 mL) full-fat coconut milk
Salt and black pepper
2 tbsp (30 mL) chopped fresh basil (optional)

1. Cook the pasta according to the package directions. Drain and set aside, reserving the pot.

2. Return the pot to medium heat. Add the vegan butter and heat for about 1 minute, until melted. Add the onion and garlic; cook for about 5 minutes, stirring frequently, until the onion is translucent.

3. Add the vodka and marinara sauce; simmer for about 10 minutes, stirring occasionally, until the sauce has thickened slightly.

4. Add the coconut milk; stir to combine. Reduce the heat to medium-low and simmer for about 10 minutes, stirring occasionally, until the sauce has thickened. Add the cooked pasta and stir to coat.

5. Sprinkle with salt and pepper to taste. Top with basil (if using); serve.

my tip Marinara sauce is typically vegan, but make sure to check the label before buying.

zucchini boats

SERVES 2 · **5** · TIME: 1 HOUR 30 MINUTES

These zucchini boats are a big hit in my house. They never get boring because you can change up the filling every time (see my tip). It's also a really easy recipe to double.

⅓ cup (75 mL) short-grain brown rice

2 medium zucchini, halved lengthwise

1 tbsp (15 mL) vegetable oil

1 cup (250 mL) diced mushrooms

¾ cup (175 mL) store-bought marinara sauce

Salt and black pepper

½ cup (125 mL) vegan mozzarella cheese shreds

8-cup (2 L) rectangular casserole dish, lined with parchment paper

1. Cook the rice according to the package directions. Fluff with a fork and set aside.

2. Preheat the oven to 400°F (200°C).

3. Scoop out the center of each zucchini half, reserving the pulp. Place the hollowed-out zucchini boats in the prepared casserole dish and set aside. Roughly chop the reserved pulp.

4. Heat the vegetable oil in a large frying pan over medium heat. Add the mushrooms and zucchini pulp; cook for about 4 minutes, stirring frequently, until softened.

5. Add the brown rice, marinara sauce and a sprinkle of salt and pepper; stir to combine. Cook for about 5 minutes, stirring frequently, until warmed through.

6. Spoon the filling evenly into the zucchini boats. Sprinkle with vegan mozzarella cheese and pepper.

7. Bake in the preheated oven for 20 minutes, until zucchini is tender and cheese is melted. Remove from the oven and let cool slightly before serving.

> my tips You can vary this recipe by using different fillings and sauces. Try these suggestions: **GRAIN** Feel free to swap out the short-grain brown rice for an equal amount of quinoa, bulgur or another variety of rice. **VEGGIES** You can substitute the same amount of corn kernels or green peas (or a mix of both) for the mushrooms. **SAUCE** Try different flavors of marinara sauce. Some of my favorites include sweet basil, garlic & herb, and roasted red pepper.

coconut almond veg & rice bowl

SERVES 2 • **5** • TIME: 35 MINUTES

This tasty meal requires only five ingredients, which is perfect when you're low on groceries but don't want to order takeout (again). I always keep a bag of mixed frozen vegetables on hand for quick meals and recipes like this one. The sauce has only three ingredients but is super creamy, a little bit spicy and so satisfying.

1 cup (250 mL) short-grain white rice
Vegetable oil
4 cups (1 L) frozen mixed vegetables (such as carrots, broccoli, peas, corn)

1½ cups (375 mL) full-fat coconut milk
2 tbsp (30 mL) almond butter (see my tip)
2 tbsp (30 mL) Sriracha sauce
Pinch salt

1. Cook the rice according to the package directions. Fluff with a fork and set aside.

2. Meanwhile, heat 1 tbsp (15 mL) vegetable oil in a medium frying pan over medium heat. Add the veggies and cook for about 6 minutes, stirring occasionally, until heated through and starting to brown.

3. Add the coconut milk, almond butter, Sriracha sauce and a pinch of salt; stir to combine. Cook for about 3 minutes, stirring frequently, until the sauce thickens slightly.

4. Divide the cooked rice between 2 bowls and spoon the vegetables overtop; serve.

my tip You can easily substitute any smooth nut or seed butter in this recipe. Peanut butter, tahini and sunflower seed butter all work well here.

sheet-pan pot pie

SERVES 4 • ⬭ • TIME: 1 HOUR 10 MINUTES

I hope we can all agree that the best part of pot pie is the flaky golden pastry topping! This recipe provides a great topping-to-filling ratio, so you get more golden pastry with each serving. It's a great fall dish and perfect for the holidays. The taste is similar to a traditional creamy pot pie, but I use tofu instead of chicken. Don't worry, though, the tofu isn't bland, as some people might expect; it absorbs all that good herby flavor, so don't be afraid to serve it at your family dinner.

Pot Pie

3 large white potatoes, peeled and chopped

3 large carrots, chopped

2 celery stalks, chopped

½ onion, diced

1 cup (250 mL) cubed firm tofu, pressed (see my tips, page 74)

1 tbsp (15 mL) vegetable oil

Salt and black pepper

Gravy

2 tbsp (30 mL) vegan butter

2 tbsp (30 mL) all-purpose flour

1½ cups (375 mL) low-sodium vegetable broth

1 tsp (5 mL) dried thyme

Salt and black pepper

1 sheet (12 by 8½ inches/30 by 22 cm) vegan puff pastry

13- by 9-inch (33 by 23 cm) rimmed baking sheet, greased

1. Preheat the oven to 400°F (200°C).

2. **POT PIE** Place the potatoes, carrots, celery, onion and tofu on the prepared baking sheet. Drizzle with the vegetable oil and sprinkle with salt and pepper; stir gently to coat.

3. Bake in the preheated oven for 30 minutes, stirring halfway through, until the potatoes and carrots are fork-tender and the tofu is golden.

4. **GRAVY** Meanwhile, melt the vegan butter in a small pot over medium heat. Whisk in the flour. Add ¼ cup (60 mL) broth; whisk until smooth. Continue adding the broth ¼ cup (60 mL) at a time, whisking continuously and letting it thicken slightly between additions, about 10 minutes in total. Add the thyme; stir. Set aside.

5. Remove the baking sheet from the oven. Pour the gravy evenly over everything and sprinkle with salt and pepper. Unfold the vegan pastry over the top. It won't reach right to the edges, but that's okay. Poke 6 slits in the top with a sharp knife to allow steam to escape, then bake for 10 minutes, until the pastry is golden. Let cool slightly before serving.

hearty white bean & veggie stew

SERVES 4 • ⬤ • TIME: 50 MINUTES

Sometimes vegan stews can seem boring, as if they contain only sad leftover veggies found in the fridge. But trust me, this one is anything but boring! I use hearty root vegetables and white beans that are simmered in a smoky tomato-based sauce. It's perfect for those fall and winter days when it's so chilly you need to warm up from the inside out. The flavor only improves over time, so any leftovers will taste even better than on the day you made it.

1 tbsp (15 mL) vegetable oil

1 onion, diced

2 garlic cloves, minced

1 cup (250 mL) diced carrot

1 cup (250 mL) peeled and diced white potato

½ cup (125 mL) diced celery

1 tsp (5 mL) smoked paprika (see my tip)

½ tsp (2 mL) hot pepper flakes

½ tsp (2 mL) dried thyme

1 can (14 oz/398 mL) white beans, such as cannellini, drained and rinsed

1 can (28 oz/796 mL) crushed tomatoes (with juice)

1½ cups (375 mL) low-sodium vegetable broth

Salt and black pepper

2 cups (500 mL) finely chopped kale, ribs removed

1. Heat the vegetable oil in a large pot over medium heat. Add the onion and garlic; cook for about 5 minutes, stirring frequently, until the onion is translucent.

2. Add the carrot, potato, celery, smoked paprika, hot pepper flakes and thyme. Cook for about 2 minutes, stirring frequently, until vegetables are softened slightly. Add the beans, crushed tomatoes (with juice), broth and a sprinkle of salt and pepper; stir to combine. Increase the heat to medium-high and bring to a boil. Reduce the heat to medium-low, cover and simmer for about 20 minutes, stirring occasionally, until the vegetables are fork-tender.

3. Add the kale and stir for about 1 minute, until wilted. Taste and adjust salt and pepper, if desired. Serve immediately or store in an airtight container in the fridge for up to 5 days.

my tip Smoked paprika is easy to find in the spice aisle of most well-stocked grocery stores. You can also often find it in bulk food stores, which is great if you want to buy only a small amount. However, if you have only regular paprika, don't sweat it! You can substitute the same amount of regular paprika for the smoked.

sides

jalapeño cornbread muffins

MAKES 12 MUFFINS • ● • TIME: 35 MINUTES

These muffins start baking at a high temperature to give the tops a nice lift, and then you reduce the heat to finish baking them. This ensures fluffy, perfect muffins every time! I love to serve these with soup (like my Apple, Squash & Cheddar Soup, page 109) or to eat them as an afternoon snack with a thick spread of vegan butter.

1¼ cups (310 mL) cornmeal

1¼ cups (310 mL) all-purpose flour

½ cup (125 mL) lightly packed brown sugar

1 tsp (5 mL) baking powder

1 tsp (5 mL) baking soda

½ tsp (2 mL) salt

1¼ cups (310 mL) unsweetened nondairy milk

½ cup (125 mL) vegan butter, melted

1 tbsp (15 mL) white vinegar or freshly squeezed lemon juice

1 jalapeño pepper, seeded and thinly sliced

12-cup muffin tin, greased or lined with paper liners

1. Preheat the oven to 425°F (220°C).

2. Whisk together the cornmeal, flour, brown sugar, baking powder, baking soda and salt in a large bowl.

3. Add the nondairy milk, vegan butter and vinegar; stir until combined and smooth. Add the jalapeño pepper; stir to combine.

4. Spoon the batter into the prepared muffin tin, filling the cups about three-quarters full.

5. Bake in the preheated oven for 5 minutes, then reduce the temperature to 350°F (180°C) and bake for 15 minutes, until the tops are set and slightly cracked.

6. Remove from the oven and let cool for 5 minutes in the muffin tin, then transfer to a wire rack to cool completely before serving.

my tip Store the muffins in an airtight container in the fridge for up to 1 week or in the freezer for up to 3 months. **TO REHEAT FROM THE FRIDGE** Microwave on High for 20-second intervals, until warmed through. **TO REHEAT FROM THE FREEZER** Preheat the oven to 350°F (180°C). Place the frozen muffins in an oven-safe dish and cover with tinfoil. Heat in the preheated oven for 10 to 15 minutes, until warmed through.

my tip Placing a dish towel over the freshly baked loaf keeps the crust soft, like store-bought sliced bread. If you prefer a crispy crust, you can let the loaf cool without the towel over it.

classic white sandwich bread

MAKES 1 LOAF • **5** • TIME: 1 HOUR
(PLUS 1 HOUR FOR RISING)

I used to be very intimidated by the idea of making my own bread. The whole process of activating yeast and letting it rise seemed confusing and easy to mess up. However, once you get the hang of it, the process really isn't that scary. Now, more often than not, I make my own bread rather than purchase it from the store.

1 cup (250 mL) unsweetened nondairy milk

¼ cup (60 mL) organic cane sugar

1 tbsp (15 mL) active dry yeast

2 tbsp + 1 tsp (35 mL) coconut oil, melted and divided

Pinch salt

2½ cups (625 mL) all-purpose flour (approx.)

9- by 5-inch (23 by 12.5 cm) metal loaf pan, greased

1. Pour the nondairy milk into a small pot over medium heat. Heat until slightly warm to the touch.

2. Pour the nondairy milk into a large bowl. Add the sugar and whisk until dissolved. Whisk in the yeast and let stand for about 10 minutes, until a foamy layer forms on top.

3. Stir in 2 tbsp (30 mL) coconut oil and salt. Add the flour ½ cup (125 mL) at a time, stirring after each addition. Once it starts to form a dough, you can use your hands to incorporate the flour. Transfer to a lightly floured surface, reserving the bowl, and knead for 10 minutes, until the dough is smooth and elastic.

4. Wash and dry the reserved bowl, then lightly grease with 1 tsp (5 mL) coconut oil. Put the dough back in the bowl and cover with a clean dish towel. Place in a warm, draft-free environment to rise for 1 hour, until doubled in size.

5. Preheat the oven to 350°F (180°C).

6. Remove the dough from the bowl and knead on a lightly floured surface about 10 times, until a smooth ball forms. Place in the prepared loaf pan, pressing down slightly.

7. Bake in the preheated oven for about 30 minutes or until golden on top. If you knock on the top crust, it should sound hollow.

8. Remove from the oven and place a clean dish towel over the loaf (see my tip). Let cool completely in the pan, then transfer to a cutting board to slice.

roasted fall veggies with maple mustard glaze

SERVES 4 • ⬭ • TIME: 45 MINUTES

I can't get enough of these vegetables! I originally fell in love with using maple syrup and mustard together when I was working on dip ideas for a roasted vegetable recipe I was creating for a brand partnership. The dip was fabulous, but then I had an even better idea: Why not make it into a pourable glaze so every bite of vegetables is bathed in delicious maple mustard flavor?

Fall Veggies
2 medium carrots, peeled and chopped

1 large sweet potato, peeled and chopped

1 large white potato, peeled and chopped

1 tbsp (15 mL) vegetable oil

Pinch salt and black pepper

Maple Mustard Glaze
2 tbsp (30 mL) olive oil

2 tbsp (30 mL) Dijon mustard

2 tbsp (30 mL) pure maple syrup

1 tbsp (15 mL) Sriracha sauce

Optional Garnish
1 tbsp (15 mL) chopped fresh parsley

Large rimmed baking sheet, lined with parchment paper

1. Preheat the oven to 400°F (200°C).

2. **FALL VEGGIES** Place the carrots, sweet potato and white potato in a large bowl. Add the vegetable oil and sprinkle with salt and pepper; toss to coat. Spread the vegetables on the prepared baking sheet in an even layer.

3. Bake in the preheated oven for 20 minutes, until the vegetables soften slightly.

4. **MAPLE MUSTARD GLAZE** Meanwhile, whisk together the olive oil, Dijon mustard, maple syrup and Sriracha sauce in a small bowl.

5. Remove the baking sheet from the oven. Drizzle the glaze over the vegetables and gently stir to combine. Bake for about 15 minutes more, until the vegetables are fork-tender.

6. Remove the baking sheet from the oven and let the vegetables cool slightly before serving. Sprinkle with parsley (if using); serve.

cheesy stuffed tomatoes

SERVES 4 • ⬭ • TIME: 35 MINUTES

I'm not a huge tomato person when they're just playing a supporting role, say in sandwiches or burgers. However, I love when tomatoes are the star of the show in recipes such as this one. It's a very comforting dish: the crunchy, cheesy filling really complements the juiciness of the fresh tomatoes. They're a great accompaniment to my Herb Risotto with Parmesan Sprinkle (page 109).

½ cup (125 mL) panko bread crumbs
¼ cup (60 mL) lightly packed finely chopped fresh basil
¼ cup (60 mL) vegan mozzarella cheese shreds
2 tbsp (30 mL) vegan Parmesan cheese or Herb & Garlic Parmesan Sprinkle (page 27; see my tip)

¼ tsp (1 mL) garlic powder
Pinch salt
4 large plum (Roma) tomatoes, halved
Cooking spray or melted vegan butter

Large rimmed baking sheet, lined with parchment paper

1. Preheat the oven to 400°F (200°C).

2. Combine the panko crumbs, basil, vegan mozzarella cheese, vegan Parmesan, garlic powder and salt in a medium bowl.

3. Scoop out the pulp and seeds from the middle of each tomato half. Slice a small piece off the rounded side of each half so it can lie flat. Place the tomato halves on the prepared baking sheet.

4. Divide the panko mixture evenly among the tomatoes. Spray the top of each with cooking spray (or brush with melted vegan butter) to ensure it turns a nice golden brown.

5. Bake in the preheated oven for 20 to 25 minutes, until the tomatoes are tender and the topping is golden brown. Remove from the oven and let cool slightly before serving.

my tip If you're using the Herb & Garlic Parmesan Sprinkle, omit the garlic powder in this recipe.

mixed veg & white beans in spiced tahini sauce

SERVES 4 • ⬭ • TIME: 30 MINUTES

This side dish is packed with so many good veggies! I've used some of my favorites here, but feel free to substitute other vegetables you enjoy, like green beans, asparagus or even other types of mushrooms. This dish is creamy, a little spicy and super hearty. To make it a complete meal, try it over a bed of quinoa, or serve as a side with Creamy Carrot Shells (page 146) or BBQ King Oyster "Pulled Pork" Sandwiches (page 129).

1 red onion, sliced

1 zucchini, sliced

1 red bell pepper, sliced

1 cup (250 mL) sliced mushrooms

1 can (14 oz/398 mL) white beans, such as cannellini, drained and rinsed

2 tbsp (30 mL) olive oil

Salt and black pepper

1 recipe Spiced Tahini Sauce (page 182)

2 tsp (10 mL) sesame seeds

Large rimmed baking sheet, lined with parchment paper

1. Preheat the oven to 400°F (200°C).

2. Place the onion, zucchini, bell pepper, mushrooms, beans, olive oil and a sprinkle of salt and pepper in a large bowl; toss to combine.

3. Spread the vegetables on the prepared baking sheet in an even layer. Bake in the preheated oven for 10 minutes.

4. Remove from the oven, stir and bake for 5 minutes more, until the vegetables and beans are fork-tender.

5. Remove from the oven and let cool slightly. Drizzle the Spiced Tahini Sauce overtop and sprinkle with sesame seeds; serve.

all-crust scalloped potatoes

SERVES 4 TO 6 • ⬭ • TIME: 1 HOUR

These aren't your typical scalloped potatoes! Aside from being entirely vegan (there's not an ounce of dairy in sight), this recipe is prepared on a sheet pan, meaning that every bite has that golden crispy, caramelized cheesiness that is everyone's favorite part of this dish. It might look different from what you're used to, but I promise it's even better.

2 tbsp (30 mL) vegan butter
½ white onion, finely chopped
2 garlic cloves, minced
2 tbsp (30 mL) all-purpose flour
1 can (14 oz/398 mL) full-fat coconut milk
¼ cup (60 mL) water
½ tsp (2 mL) dried thyme
½ tsp (2 mL) dried parsley

½ tsp (2 mL) salt
½ tsp (2 mL) black pepper
4 large russet potatoes, peeled and sliced into ¼-inch (0.5 cm) rounds
2 cups (500 mL) shredded vegan Cheddar cheese

13- by 9-inch (33 by 23 cm) rimmed baking sheet, greased

1. Preheat the oven to 375°F (190°C). Position one oven rack 4 inches (10 cm) from the broiler.

2. Melt the vegan butter in a medium pot over medium heat. Add the onion and garlic; cook for about 5 minutes, stirring frequently, until the onion is translucent.

3. Add the flour; whisk vigorously for about 1 minute, until a thick paste forms. Immediately add the coconut milk ¼ cup (60 mL) at a time, whisking constantly until thickened, about 8 minutes total.

4. Add the water, thyme, parsley, salt and pepper; stir to combine. Simmer for about 5 minutes, stirring occasionally, until the sauce has thickened slightly.

5. Spread the potatoes on the prepared baking sheet in an even layer, with the slices overlapping slightly. Pour the sauce over the potatoes until they are covered. Sprinkle evenly with the vegan Cheddar cheese.

6. Bake on the middle rack of the preheated oven for 25 minutes, until the potatoes are fork-tender and the cheese has melted.

7. Turn the oven to Broil and move the baking sheet to the top rack. Broil for 3 to 5 minutes, until the potatoes are golden and crisp. Remove from the oven and let cool slightly before serving.

garlicky ginger baby bok choy

SERVES 4 • **5** • TIME: 15 MINUTES

Bok choy is my favorite vegetable — I buy it pretty much every week. Sometimes I add it to stir-fries, but most often I use it for this delicious side dish. The smell of fresh garlic and ginger cooking is so irresistible that it's a good thing this is a quick recipe. Otherwise you would be tempted to start eating it right from the pan! It's a great side dish with my "Honey" Garlic Tofu & Broccoli (page 154) and some rice.

2 tbsp (30 mL) coconut oil
or canola oil

1-inch (2.5 cm) piece ginger,
finely chopped

2 garlic cloves, minced

6 heads baby bok choy,
quartered

1 tbsp (15 mL) water

1 tbsp (15 mL) reduced-sodium
soy sauce

1. Heat the coconut oil in a large frying pan over medium heat. Add the ginger and garlic; cook for about 3 minutes, stirring frequently, until starting to brown.

2. Add the bok choy and cook for 2 minutes, stirring frequently, until slightly softened.

3. Add the water and soy sauce. Cover the frying pan with a lid and cook for about 3 minutes, until the bok choy is fork-tender.

4. Remove from the heat and let cool slightly before serving.

spicy oven-roasted corn on the cob

SERVES 4 • ⬦ • TIME: 35 MINUTES

Corn on the cob reminds me of August dinners at our cottage in Prince Edward Island. My family always just boiled the corn and served it with butter (vegan butter for me, of course), but I recently started playing around with different ways to enjoy corn on the cob at home, and this spicy version is so good! I love that it's mostly hands-off and gets such an amazing roasted flavor in the oven. It's the perfect side for BBQ King Oyster "Pulled Pork" sandwiches (page 129) or Grown-Up Nuggets & Fries (page 145).

¼ cup (60 mL) melted vegan butter

2 tsp (10 mL) chili powder

1 tsp (5 mL) ground cumin

½ tsp (2 mL) smoked paprika (see my tip, page 72)

¼ tsp (1 mL) garlic powder

¼ tsp (1 mL) onion powder

½ tsp (2 mL) salt

4 fresh corn ears, husked and halved crosswise

Rimmed baking sheet, lined with parchment paper

1. Preheat the oven to 425°F (220°C).

2. Combine the melted vegan butter, chili powder, cumin, smoked paprika, garlic powder, onion powder and salt in a small bowl. Reserve one-quarter of the mixture and set aside.

3. Place the corn on the prepared baking sheet. Evenly brush each piece with the vegan butter mixture.

4. Bake in the preheated oven for 15 minutes. Remove from the oven, flip the pieces and brush the reserved vegan butter mixture overtop. Bake for 10 minutes more or until tender and starting to brown on top.

5. Remove from the oven and let cool slightly before serving.

leftover grains & cauliflower tray bake

SERVES 4 • ⬤ • TIME: 35 MINUTES

This is my current favorite way to use leftover rice or quinoa. I don't know about you, but I hate that leftover grains always get a bit sad and firm in the fridge; they're never quite as fluffy as when freshly made. However, for this recipe they don't need to be. Everything is baked together on a sheet pan, and the grains get a lovely, slightly crispy texture that pairs perfectly with the roasted cauliflower and lentils.

1 large cauliflower head, chopped into bite-size florets

½ onion, finely chopped

2 garlic cloves, minced

2 tbsp (30 mL) vegetable oil

1 tbsp (15 mL) curry powder

1 tsp (5 mL) ground cumin

1 tsp (5 mL) paprika

Salt and black pepper

1½ cups (375 mL) cooked brown lentils, drained and rinsed

1¼ cups (310 mL) cooked rice or quinoa

½ cup (125 mL) golden raisins

¼ cup (60 mL) chopped fresh cilantro

Large rimmed baking sheet, lined with parchment paper

1. Preheat the oven to 400°F (200°C).

2. Place the cauliflower, onion, garlic, vegetable oil, curry powder, cumin, paprika and a sprinkle of salt and pepper in a large bowl; toss to combine.

3. Spread the cauliflower mixture on the prepared baking sheet in an even layer, reserving the bowl. Bake in the preheated oven for 15 minutes.

4. Remove the baking sheet from the oven. Add the lentils, rice, raisins and a sprinkle of salt and pepper; stir gently to combine. Bake for 10 minutes more, until the cauliflower is fork-tender.

5. Remove from the oven and let cool slightly. Top with cilantro and extra salt and pepper, if desired. Serve.

back-pocket broccoli

SERVES 4 • ⬭ 5 • TIME: 20 MINUTES

This is a super-simple dish that somehow tastes incredible. It's become a bit of a back-pocket recipe for me: a trusty side I turn to when I can't think of what else to make. The broccoli is oven-baked to crisp perfection, and because it's slightly charred, it has a smoky flavor that balances the salty nutritional yeast. Make this recipe to go with Simple Squash Risotto (page 140) or Eggplant Parm (page 158) for a delicious plant-powered dinner.

1 large broccoli head, chopped into florets
2 tbsp (30 mL) vegetable oil
1 tbsp (15 mL) nutritional yeast
¼ tsp (1 mL) garlic powder
Salt and black pepper

1 tsp (5 mL) freshly squeezed lemon juice

Large rimmed baking sheet, lined with parchment paper

1. Preheat the oven to 450°F (230°C).

2. Place the broccoli in a large bowl. Add the vegetable oil, nutritional yeast, garlic powder and a sprinkle of salt and pepper; toss to combine.

3. Spread the broccoli on the prepared baking sheet in an even layer. Bake in the preheated oven for 10 minutes, until the broccoli starts to brown.

4. Remove the baking sheet from the oven, flip the broccoli and cook for 2 minutes more, until fork-tender.

5. Remove from the oven and sprinkle with salt and pepper. Drizzle with lemon juice; serve.

my tip If you want to add some spiciness, add ¼ tsp (1 mL) cayenne pepper in Step 2.

dad's holiday red cabbage

SERVES 8 • ⬤ • TIME: 1 HOUR 50 MINUTES

I had to put "holiday" in the title of this recipe because that's the only time my dad makes this! It's likely his German roots, but he always says a holiday dinner isn't complete without red cabbage. It took me a few Christmases to come around to this tangy, salty side dish that's reminiscent of sauerkraut, but now I wholeheartedly agree with him and always add some to my plate!

1 tbsp (15 mL) vegetable oil
1 green apple, peeled and finely diced
¼ cup (60 mL) onion, finely chopped
1 medium head red cabbage, thinly sliced (about 5 cups/1.25 L)

⅓ cup (75 mL) apple cider vinegar
¼ cup (60 mL) organic cane sugar
1 tsp (5 mL) salt
¼ tsp (1 mL) ground cloves
Black pepper

1. Heat the vegetable oil in a large pot over medium heat. Add the apple and onion; cook for about 5 minutes, stirring occasionally, until the onion is translucent and the apple has softened slightly.

2. Add the cabbage, vinegar, sugar, salt, cloves and a sprinkle of pepper; stir to combine. Bring to a boil, then reduce the heat to low and simmer for 1½ hours, stirring occasionally, until the cabbage is very soft and the volume is reduced by about half.

3. Transfer to a serving dish and let cool slightly before serving.

my tip This recipe is best made the day of, but the good news is, most of the cooking time is hands-off, freeing you up to enjoy friends and family.

perfect pressure cooker lentils

SERVES 8 • • TIME: 30 MINUTES

These lentils are a great potluck side dish to accompany any plant-based meal. They're slightly spicy and reminiscent of chili. This recipe makes enough to feed a crowd, but if you find there's too much, you can freeze the leftovers to enjoy at a later date. This is also a great make-ahead recipe (see my tips for instructions).

1 can (28 oz/796 mL) diced tomatoes (with juice)

2 cups (500 mL) reduced-sodium vegetable broth

1½ cups (375 mL) dried brown or green lentils

2 tsp (10 mL) ground cumin

2 tsp (10 mL) chili powder

1 tsp (5 mL) onion powder

½ tsp (2 mL) garlic powder

1 tsp (5 mL) salt (approx.)

½ tsp (2 mL) black pepper (approx.)

Electric pressure cooker

1. Combine the tomatoes (with juice), broth, lentils, cumin, chili powder, onion powder, garlic powder and salt in the pressure cooker pot. Secure the lid and cook on high pressure for 12 minutes.

2. Once the cooking is finished, quick-release the pressure. Let stand with the lid on for 5 minutes.

3. Remove the lid, stir and season with additional salt and pepper, if desired.

my tips **MAKE-AHEAD** Prepare through Step 3 and let cool slightly. Transfer to an airtight container and store in the fridge until ready to use, up to 4 days. To reheat, place the lentils in a large pot over medium heat; cook, stirring frequently, for about 5 minutes, until warm. **FREEZING** Store leftovers in an airtight container in the freezer for up to 3 months. To reheat, thaw overnight in the fridge. Place the lentils in a large pot over medium heat; cook, stirring frequently, for about 5 minutes, until warm.

lemon sesame green beans

SERVES 4 • 5 • TIME: 15 MINUTES

This recipe was kind of a happy accident. I couldn't decide if I wanted a strong salty sesame flavor for my green beans or more of a fresh "just a squeeze of lemon" vibe, so I decided to do both. The result was deliciously tangy and slightly nutty-tasting green beans. These are great served with Liv's Popcorn Chick'n (page 80) and Grown-Up Nuggets & Fries (page 145).

12 ounces (375 g) frozen green beans (see my tips)

2 tbsp (30 mL) reduced-sodium soy sauce

2 tsp (10 mL) sesame oil

1 tsp (5 mL) freshly squeezed lemon juice (see my tips)

Salt and black pepper

1. Place the green beans in a large frying pan. Cook over medium heat for about 5 minutes, stirring occasionally, until slightly softened.

2. Add the soy sauce, sesame oil and lemon juice; stir to coat. Cook for 3 minutes, stirring frequently, until the beans start to brown.

3. Remove from the heat and sprinkle with salt and pepper. Serve.

my tips You can also use the same quantity of trimmed fresh green beans for this recipe. Bring a medium pot of water to a boil. Add the green beans and cook for 3 minutes, until bright green and tender-crisp. Drain and proceed with the recipe as directed.

If you prefer a tarter flavor, add another ½ tsp (2 mL) freshly squeezed lemon juice.

desserts

apple blackberry crisp

SERVES 4 TO 6 • ⬤ • TIME: 1 HOUR

My extended family used to take a trip to Maine every summer, staying in a cottage on the coast. Of course, as a diehard sweets person, one of my favorite memories of those years is my Aunty V's homemade apple and blackberry crisp. It was an unusual combination (I had never seen apples and blackberries together before), but perfectly sweet with a crispy golden brown top — perfect with a scoop of vanilla ice cream. It was so delicious I knew I had to create a vegan version!

3 cups (750 mL) peeled and diced baking apples (about 3 large; see my tips)

1 cup (250 mL) fresh blackberries

⅓ cup (75 mL) lightly packed brown sugar, divided

1 tbsp (15 mL) freshly squeezed lemon juice

2 tsp (10 mL) ground cinnamon

1¼ cups (310 mL) large-flake (old-fashioned) rolled oats

⅓ cup (75 mL) vegan butter

Vegan vanilla ice cream

6-cup (1.5 L) casserole dish, greased

Pastry blender (optional)

1. Preheat the oven to 350°F (180°C).

2. Place the apples, blackberries, 1 tbsp (15 mL) brown sugar, lemon juice and cinnamon in a large bowl; stir gently to coat. Pour into the prepared casserole dish, reserving the bowl. Set aside.

3. Combine the oats and remaining ¼ cup (60 mL) brown sugar in the reserved bowl. Using two knives or a pastry blender, cut the vegan butter into the oat mixture until crumbly.

4. Spread the oat topping evenly over the fruit mixture. Bake in the preheated oven for 35 to 40 minutes, until the top is golden brown.

5. Remove from the oven and let cool for 5 to 10 minutes. Serve warm with a scoop of vegan vanilla ice cream on top.

my tips Some apples are better for eating and some are better for baking. The best baking apples are ones that hold their shape when cooked, such as Cortland, Honeycrisp and Granny Smith.

Cover the casserole dish or transfer leftovers to an airtight container and store in the fridge for up to 3 days.

coconut & maple banana cake

SERVES 9 • ⬤ • TIME: 45 MINUTES

You never need a reason for cake, but when I make a "just because" cake, I don't want it to take a ton of time or effort. This recipe is beyond easy and takes less than an hour to whip up. I use coconut yogurt instead of oil here to provide the moisture and to add a delicious coconut flavor!

3 large overripe bananas, mashed
½ cup (125 mL) vegan coconut yogurt
¼ cup (60 mL) pure maple syrup
1 tsp (5 mL) vanilla extract
1½ cups (375 mL) all-purpose flour
1 tsp (5 mL) baking powder

1 tsp (5 mL) baking soda
½ tsp (2 mL) ground cinnamon
½ tsp (2 mL) salt

8-inch (20 cm) square metal baking pan, lined with parchment paper

1. Preheat the oven to 350°F (180°C).

2. Place the mashed bananas in a large bowl. Add the vegan coconut yogurt, maple syrup and vanilla; stir well to combine.

3. Add the flour, baking powder, baking soda, cinnamon and salt; stir until combined. The batter will be thick.

4. Spread into the prepared pan. Bake in the preheated oven for 33 to 35 minutes or until a toothpick inserted in the center comes out clean and the top is golden and slightly cracked.

5. Remove from the oven and let cool completely in the pan. Slice and serve. Store in an airtight container at room temperature for up to 3 days or in the fridge for up to 5 days.

my tip This cake is delicious as is, but take it up a notch by adding a layer of Classic Chocolate Frosting (page 34) once it's fully cooled.

soft & gooey oatmeal raisin cookies

Some people like their oatmeal cookies crispy, but I prefer mine super soft and gooey. I like raisins in this recipe, but if vegan chocolate chips are more your style, feel free to substitute those instead.

1 cup (250 mL) lightly packed brown sugar

½ cup (125 mL) soft vegan margarine (see my tip)

2 tbsp (30 mL) unsweetened nondairy milk

1 tbsp (15 mL) light (fancy) molasses

2 tsp (10 mL) vanilla extract

¾ cup (175 mL) all-purpose flour

½ tsp (2 mL) baking powder

½ tsp (2 mL) baking soda

½ tsp (2 mL) ground cinnamon

¼ tsp (1 mL) salt

1¼ cups (310 mL) large-flake (old-fashioned) rolled oats

½ cup (125 mL) raisins

Large baking sheet, lined with parchment paper

1. Cream together the brown sugar and vegan margarine in a large bowl. Beat until light and fluffy, about 2 minutes. Add the nondairy milk, molasses and vanilla; beat until incorporated.

2. Add the flour, baking powder, baking soda, cinnamon and salt; stir to combine. Add the oats and raisins; stir until combined. Cover and refrigerate for at least 1 hour or up to 3 days.

3. Preheat the oven to 350°F (180°C).

4. Spoon 1½ tbsp (22 mL) dough for each cookie onto the prepared baking sheet, spacing at least 2 inches (5 cm) apart.

5. Bake in the preheated oven for 10 minutes, until golden on top.

6. Remove from the oven. Let cool on the baking sheet for 10 minutes. Transfer to a wire rack for at least 5 minutes. Serve warm or let cool completely and store in an airtight container at room temperature for up to 5 days.

my tip If you can't find soft vegan margarine, you can substitute an equal amount of softened vegan butter or coconut oil, plus an additional 2 tbsp (30 mL) unsweetened nondairy milk.

pumpkin pie–stuffed sticky rolls

MAKES 20 ROLLS • ⬭ • TIME: 1 HOUR 15 MINUTES
(PLUS 1 HOUR FOR RISING)

I can't think of anything more satisfying on a chilly fall afternoon than a sheet pan packed to the brim with these sticky rolls. If you love pumpkin-spiced lattes, this might just be the sweet treat for you! The creamy pumpkin purée is flavored with cinnamon, nutmeg and brown sugar, then rolled up in fluffy cinnamon-bun dough. During October and November I'm pretty much in a "pumpkin everything" mood, and these rolls are a recipe I come back to every autumn.

Sticky Rolls

2 cups (500 mL) unsweetened nondairy milk

6 tbsp (90 mL) organic cane sugar

2 tsp (10 mL) active dry yeast

6 tbsp (90 mL) vegan butter, melted

4½ cups (1.125 L) all-purpose flour (approx.)

Vegetable oil

Pumpkin Pie Filling

½ cup (125 mL) vegan butter

½ cup (125 mL) canned pumpkin purée

1 cup (250 mL) lightly packed brown sugar

2 tbsp (30 mL) ground cinnamon

¼ tsp (1 mL) ground nutmeg

13- by 9-inch (33 by 23 cm) rimmed baking sheet, lined with parchment paper

1. **STICKY ROLLS** Place the nondairy milk and sugar in a small pot over medium heat. Heat, stirring frequently, until the sugar has dissolved and the mixture is warm to the touch. Pour into a large bowl and sprinkle the yeast evenly overtop. Set aside for 10 minutes, until foamy on top.

2. Add the vegan butter and 1½ cups (375 mL) flour; stir. Add remaining flour 1½ cups (375 mL) at a time, stirring after each addition. Once it starts to form a dough, you can use your hands to incorporate all the flour. Transfer to a lightly floured surface, reserving the bowl, and knead for about 30 seconds, until a smooth ball forms.

3. Wash and dry the reserved bowl, then lightly grease with vegetable oil. Put the dough back in the bowl and cover with a clean dish towel. Place in a warm, draft-free environment for 1 hour, until doubled in size.

4. **PUMPKIN PIE FILLING** Meanwhile, combine the vegan butter, pumpkin purée, brown sugar, cinnamon and nutmeg; beat for about 1 minute, until combined and fluffy.

CONTINUED ON PAGE 208

5. Preheat the oven to 375°F (190°C).

6. Transfer the dough to a lightly floured surface. Using a rolling pin, roll the dough into a rectangle about 24 inches (60 cm) long by 18 inches (45 cm) wide. Spread the filling evenly over the dough. Starting with the long side closest to you, roll the dough from bottom to top, ensuring that it stays tight.

7. Slice the roll into twenty 1-inch (2.5 cm) pieces and place on the prepared baking sheet (they will touch, but that's okay). Bake in the preheated oven for 24 to 26 minutes, until golden brown on top and the filling is bubbling.

8. Remove from the oven and let cool slightly before serving. Store in an airtight container at room temperature for up to 3 days or in the freezer for up to 3 months.

my tips To make a super simple glaze for these sticky rolls, add 2 cups (500 mL) confectioners' (icing) sugar and 3 tbsp (45 mL) unsweetened nondairy milk to a large bowl and whisk until combined.

Extra pumpkin purée? No problem! You can store it in an airtight container in the fridge for up to 1 week or freeze it for up to 3 months.

gluten-free coconut butter brownies

These brownies are shockingly delicious, despite how simple they are. I typically shy away from gluten-free baked goods, since I don't need to avoid gluten. I usually find they are too dry for my liking, but these brownies are so fudgy — thanks to the coconut butter — that you would never know they don't contain gluten, dairy or eggs!

1¾ cups (425 mL) light buckwheat flour (see my tips)

1¼ cups (310 mL) organic cane sugar

½ cup (125 mL) unsweetened cocoa powder

1 tsp (5 mL) baking soda

Pinch salt

1 cup (250 mL) unsweetened nondairy milk

¾ cup (175 mL) store-bought coconut butter or Creamy Coconut Butter (page 32), melted (see my tips)

1 tsp (5 mL) vanilla extract

1½ cups (375 mL) store-bought vegan chocolate frosting or 1 recipe Classic Chocolate Frosting (page 34)

8-inch (20 cm) square metal baking pan, lined with parchment paper

1. Preheat the oven to 350°F (180°C).

2. Whisk together the buckwheat flour, sugar, cocoa powder, baking soda and salt in a large bowl.

3. Add the nondairy milk, coconut butter and vanilla. Stir to form a dough. The batter will be very thick and not runny.

4. Press into the prepared baking pan. Bake in the preheated oven for 32 to 34 minutes, until a toothpick inserted in the center comes out clean.

5. Remove from the oven and let cool completely in the pan. Using a knife, spread the vegan frosting evenly over the brownies. Slice and serve. Store in an airtight container at room temperature for up to 4 days.

my tips Make sure to use light buckwheat flour in this recipe. Regular or dark buckwheat flour will have a bitter, earthy taste and a grainy consistency. You can find the light version at most well-stocked grocery stores, bulk food stores and online.

Coconut butter tends to solidify at room temperature. To soften it, place the jar in a bowl of hot water and let stand for 10 minutes, until runny.

chocolate soufflé cake

SERVES 8 • **5** • TIME: 40 MINUTES

This cake is amazing for entertaining because it is crazy-easy to make and your guests will never guess it has only five ingredients! The texture is light but still decadent, and rich in chocolate flavor. I love serving it with a big dollop of sweet coconut whipped cream and fresh berries.

1⅔ cups (400 mL) all-purpose flour

1 cup (250 mL) organic cane sugar

⅔ cup (150 mL) unsweetened cocoa powder (see my tips)

1 tsp (5 mL) baking powder

Pinch salt

2 cups (500 mL) boiling water

½ cup (125 mL) canola oil

8-inch (20 cm) round cake pan, lined with parchment

1. Preheat the oven to 350°F (180°C).

2. Whisk together the flour, sugar, cocoa powder, baking powder and salt. Add the water and canola oil; stir to combine. The batter should be fairly smooth, but a few small lumps are okay.

3. Pour the batter into the prepared cake pan. Bake in the preheated oven for 30 minutes or until the top is set and a toothpick inserted in the center comes out clean. Let cool completely before slicing and serving.

my tips For an Instagram-worthy presentation, sprinkle a dusting of unsweetened cocoa powder over the top just before serving.

This cake is best made and served on the same day. However, leftovers can be stored in an airtight container in the fridge for up to 3 days.

double blueberry cinnamon crumble bars

MAKES 20 BARS • ⬭ • TIME: 1 HOUR 15 MINUTES

These crumble bars make a great dessert as well as an afternoon snack with a decaf latte. I love to make an extra batch in August, when wild blueberries are in season here in Nova Scotia, and freeze the bars so I can have them later in the fall, when I'm missing summer (see my tip).

1½ cups (375 mL) lightly packed brown sugar

1½ cups (375 mL) vegan butter, softened

½ cup (125 mL) smooth almond butter

3 cups (750 mL) all-purpose flour

1 cup (250 mL) large-flake (old-fashioned) rolled oats

1½ tsp (7 mL) ground cinnamon

½ tsp (2 mL) salt

3 cups (750 mL) fresh or frozen wild blueberries (thawed if frozen)

¾ cup (175 mL) blueberry jam

Electric mixer

13- by 9-inch (33 by 23 cm) rimmed baking sheet, lined with parchment paper

1. Preheat the oven to 350°F (180°C).

2. Place the brown sugar, vegan butter and almond butter in a large bowl; beat using an electric mixer for about 1 minute, until combined. Add the flour, oats, cinnamon and salt; stir to combine. The mixture will be slightly dry-looking and crumbly.

3. Firmly press half the oat mixture into the prepared baking pan. Evenly spread the blueberries overtop. Add 1-tsp (5 mL) dollops of jam evenly over the blueberries. Sprinkle the remaining oat mixture over everything.

4. Bake in the preheated oven for about 45 minutes or until the top is golden brown. Let cool slightly in the pan before slicing and serving. Store leftovers in an airtight container at room temperature for 4 days or in the fridge for up to 1 week.

my tip These bars freeze really well. Store the sliced bars in an airtight container or freezer bag in the freezer for up to 3 months. When ready to eat, pop out one (or a few) and microwave on Medium in 20-second intervals, until warm.

london fog sheet-pan cake

SERVES 6 TO 8 • ⬦ • TIME: 40 MINUTES

I can't believe sheet-pan cakes aren't more popular. I mean, sure, they lack height, but they more than make up for that in ease and time. With less baking time, less cooling time and less fuss, you'll want to start making all your cakes sheet-pan style. This cake was inspired by the London Fog, one of my favorite coffee-shop drinks, which is Earl Grey tea with vanilla syrup and steamed milk. Yum!

2½ cups (625 mL) all-purpose flour
2 tsp (10 mL) loose Earl Grey tea
1½ tsp (7 mL) baking soda
½ tsp (2 mL) salt
1½ cups (375 mL) organic cane sugar
1½ cups (375 mL) unsweetened nondairy milk
1 cup (250 mL) brewed Earl Grey tea, cooled
½ cup (125 mL) canola oil

1 tbsp (15 mL) vanilla extract
1 tbsp (15 mL) white vinegar
2 cups (500 mL) store-bought vegan vanilla frosting (see my tip) or 1 recipe Vanilla Buttercream (page 33)

Electric mixer

13- by 9-inch (33 by 23 cm) rimmed baking sheet, lined with parchment paper

1. Preheat the oven to 350°F (180°C).

2. Whisk together the flour, loose tea, baking soda and salt in a large bowl.

3. Place the sugar, nondairy milk, brewed tea, canola oil, vanilla and vinegar in a medium bowl. Stir until combined and the sugar is dissolved.

4. Pour the liquid mixture into the flour mixture; stir gently until just combined. Do not overmix — some small lumps are okay.

5. Pour onto the prepared baking sheet and spread in an even layer. Bake in the preheated oven for 18 to 20 minutes or until a toothpick inserted in the center comes out clean.

6. Remove the cake from the oven and let cool completely on the baking sheet. Using a knife, spread the frosting evenly overtop. Slice and serve. Store in an airtight container at room temperature for up to 4 days.

my tip A lot of store-bought frostings don't contain dairy and are therefore accidentally vegan! Make sure to check the ingredients before purchasing.

acknowledgments

When I wrote my first book, I had no idea if I would have the opportunity to do a second. I feel so lucky to be able to share my recipes again with people all over the world, and create such a special sequel to my first cookbook. There are so many people who make publishing a book possible, so I want to take a moment to extend my sincerest gratitude to you all.

Thank you to the Robert Rose team, Robert, Meredith, Megan, Rachel and Parisa for giving me the opportunity to publish a second book. I am so grateful for all the hard work you put into this book, especially during such uncertain and rocky times. Thank you to my copyeditor Gillian for polishing the manuscript and to Kelly for proofreading. And to the incredibly talented and creative photographer and food stylist, Ashley, and designer Margaux for bringing the recipes to life and capturing them in such a beautiful way.

To Mom, Dad, Bridget and Greg: thank you for your ongoing support and excitement as I pursue my dreams.

To my YouTube subscribers and online community: thank you for making my recipes, sending me the sweetest messages and making even the hard days worthwhile. You are the reason I do what I do and I am so grateful for you all.

And last but not least, thank you to my dogs, Willa and Hazel, for keeping me company in the kitchen during the long days of recipe testing and development.

index